WHO SAYS
I'm Not Good Enough?

WHO SAYS
I'm Not Good Enough?

Never Let Anyone Dim Your Light

CAROL LUMSDEN

XULON ELITE

Xulon Press Elite
2301 Lucien Way #415
Maitland, FL 32751
407.339.4217
www.xulonpress.com

© 2021 by Carol Lumsden

All rights reserved solely by the author. The author guarantees all contents are original and do not infringe upon the legal rights of any other person or work. No part of this book may be reproduced in any form without the permission of the author. The views expressed in this book are not necessarily those of the publisher.

Due to the changing nature of the Internet, if there are any web addresses, links, or URLs included in this manuscript, these may have been altered and may no longer be accessible. The views and opinions shared in this book belong solely to the author and do not necessarily reflect those of the publisher. The publisher therefore disclaims responsibility for the views or opinions expressed within the work.

Unless otherwise indicated, Scripture quotations taken from the Holy Bible, New International Version (NIV). Copyright © 1973, 1978, 1984, 2011 by Biblica, Inc.™. Used by permission. All rights reserved.

Paperback ISBN-13: 978-1-6628-3809-5
Ebook ISBN-13: 978-1-6628-3810-1

Table of Contents

Chapter 1 *Learning to Listen with Our Hearts*........1

Chapter 2 *The Farm Girl from South Africa: My Story*...............................17

Chapter 3 *Never Let Anyone Dim Your Light*........31

Chapter 4 *My Fears and Insecurities* 43

Chapter 5 *What Happened to Me* 53

Chapter 6 *The Stuff That Holds Us Back* 59

Chapter 7 *"Getting It," Getting Unstuck, and Picking Up the Pieces* 69

Chapter 8 *Looking Back and Moving Forward*.......77

Chapter 9 *Coming Full Circle*..................... 83

About the Author.................................. 99

Endnotes... 101

Acknowledgements

In loving memory of my parents Douglas and Sylvia Lumsden. I will forever be grateful for the selfless sacrifices they made for the five of us children. How they did it all for all those years still amazes me. Their love for us, their undeniable faith, service and devotion to our Lord and Savior has always been such an amazing example to us all.

In loving memory of our granny Grace and Poppah, who showed us too, how to live our lives with love, integrity, gentleness, kindness and service to our Lord. In loving memory to our brother Tom, who bravely fought brain cancer not once, but twice, never complaining and never asking "why me?" His faith and courage are something we can all aspire to live up to. I know without a doubt that we will all be together in our heavenly home one day.

I will always be grateful to my husband Gerrit, who has supported me for the many years it has taken me to write this book. Thank you for your love, patience and encouragement. Thank you for doing without while supporting me. Thank you for your example of selfless service, love and devotion to our Lord and Savior. I can only aspire to be half as devoted as you are. To all my family and friends who have been wonderful role models and so supportive all these years. You know who you are. Thank you!

I would be most remiss if I did not name my precious friend Beverly Lee. Thank you, Miss Bevels, for your unbelievable patience, getting us girls through our Midwifery exams some forty plus years ago! If you hadn't kept us awake until *dawn*, going over the work again and again until you were satisfied that *we* knew it well enough, we surely wouldn't have graduated as midwives! You instilled a life-long desire in me to learn.

My thanks to Lynne Smith at the Institute for Writers for your support, encouragement and invaluable information. You inspired me to continue writing and never give up!

Many thanks to my Editor Vanessa at Xulon Press. I was ready to end this journey until you sent back my Manuscript Review. You really 'got' my message. Thank you for your wonderful review, encouragement, and hard work editing my book!

Thank you to my Publishers, Xulon Press for being so patient all these years, waiting for me to complete my book, and for putting it all together so beautifully. I could never have done it without you all!

Introduction

I was a very sensitive and insecure child growing up, with no confidence and extremely low self-esteem. I believe that my lack of confidence has held me back a lot in my life, and I have not achieved what I wanted to. I had a long career in nursing, but it was a career with many disappointments. I worked very hard and in many ways was told that I was very competent, but that too had its drawbacks because sadly, there are many bullies in nursing, and nurses feel threatened if a colleague is knowledgeable and competent. I saw the same with many other accomplished nurses too.

I can definitely attribute some of my unhappiness to the fact that I never wanted to be a nurse and because I had felt a calling to do other things. I tried other avenues but always pulled back before I was successful in any of the endeavors. I believe a lot had to do with fear but also because I never felt "good enough." Voices and chatter of self-criticism in my head told me constantly that I was delusional to even dare think I could be a successful in another career or in business. I was also afraid of people being critical, derisive, and belittling, and to me, failing would be worse than not attempting it. I spent thousands of dollars trying to improve myself, only to find that I would land back in the same place I had been before. Each time I felt worse because I had wasted all this money and was no better off than when I had started. With added remorse and self-disgust, I knew I was sinking lower and lower into that self-imposed pit of despair, as I called it. I am the first person to admit that some of my unhappiness was self-imposed because at times, I was told that I "had what it takes" outside of nursing, but I would always abandon my dreams and run the other way.

Not having the confidence to stand up to the nasty ones who bullied me, I allowed the bullying to happen year after year until I eventually retired from nursing at one of the lowest times of my life. I had been through low times during my career, as many of us do, but to end a long career like this was devastating, and it really put me into a very dark place. Instead of celebrating my retirement from all those years of nursing, I felt sad, exhausted, defeated, and broken.

For many years, I had felt a calling to write and speak, and once again, there were the many courses, seminars, classes, and more money—more dreams either put on the backburner or dropped and forgotten altogether.

One day, I decided to really focus on the dreams and aspirations I had put on hold. I was tired and desperate to change my career. It meant re-starting a writing course, which meant more money. This course was by far one of the hardest courses I have ever done, but Lynne, my instructor, was so supportive and encouraging that after I finally completed the course, I decided I would sit down and finish this book I had started writing a number of years before.

Introduction

As soon as I started again, all the same old feelings of self-doubt came flooding back, and I just stopped. Gone were the rekindled dreams and hopes, and all those familiar, awful feelings of worthlessness crept back in.

In 2017, I was doing some work for a private company, and the president of the company asked me what I wanted to do with my future. I mentioned that I was desperate to get out of nursing and had felt called to write a book and that I had actually started writing it but did not think I had suitable material to offer anyone. Michelle surprised me when she asked me to send her some of the chapters I had already written. I was terrified and horrified at the same time, thinking that she would laugh at me, but I was so desperate that I sent her two of my stories.

She told me that she believed I had a message to share and that I *had* to complete my book. She felt that someone could learn and benefit from my pain. I was so excited that I wrote for hours the next few days. A few nights later as I lay awake in bed in the quiet darkness, the familiar chatter of voices came back. Doubt crept in as it had so many times before, and my writing came to a grinding halt. But she persisted, and one day out of the blue asked me how my book was coming on. I told her that I was ready to rip up my manuscript. She replied that if I did in fact rip it up, she would "revoke our working together" and made me promise I would send her the outline of my book by the end of that weekend. I did, and this time, her feedback was so positive that I decided to take her advice, improve on the outline, and really get down to serious writing.

I had also become more committed to reading my Bible and was constantly reading books by Christian writers. I was starting to believe that I might possibly have a message to share with women and young girls struggling with low self-confidence, low self-esteem, and feelings of unworthiness. Once again, I promised myself I would push on and complete this book.

Focusing on my past, I have learned so much about myself along the way. It really has been helpful. I've learned where I believe my insecurities came from and how I am responsible for all my failures. I have also learned that we have an amazing, loving, patient, and forgiving God, and it is our duty and purpose to share His love by helping and supporting His beloved children.

You, the reader, will find out that my life has been very different from people who have grown up here in America. But the real message is about our God who loves us and accepts us just as we are, with *all* our differences, *all* our failings, and *all* our shortcomings. It doesn't matter where we grew up; God is there for each and every one who calls on Him.

I invite you to join me on my journey. I will share with you how I did a slow, meticulous search through my past, trying to dredge up and deal with every painful memory that I prayed God would bring to my mind so I could understand my failings and insecurities and heal and move on. Some of my stories will pale in comparison with what you might be going through, but the issues were real to me, even if some of them might have been perceived beliefs I had. They were still real to me. My story is different, but it might just help you or a loved one struggling to find hope in this very different and often very toxic world.

Most of all, it is a book about getting to know what a wonderful, loving, and forgiving God we have, a book about learning to have faith in His love and not allowing *anyone* to *ever* tell you that you are not good enough or that you are a lesser person than anyone else. Who are *they* to tell you that? We are *all* children of God—created by Him, for Him, in His image. We are all created lovingly and for a purpose. It is my hope that you learn to believe that.

> "How great is the love the Father has lavished on us, that we should be called children of God! And that is what we are! The reason the world does not know us is that it did not know him." (1 John 3: 1 NIV)

CHAPTER 1

Learning to Listen with Our Hearts

It was one o'clock in the morning on a dark, cold night in a very remote part of South Africa. The area was so remote that we had no electricity, no lights to turn on.

I was twelve years old, fast asleep under a mound of blankets. Suddenly, I woke up with a jolt as my mom walked slowly into my bedroom. She was holding a candle in her one hand and shielding the flame with the other. The candle was casting weird shadows onto the wall. For a moment, I was confused. *Why is Mom coming into my room in the middle of the night? What's wrong?* I wondered.

Then with a jolt and a sick feeling in my stomach, I remembered. It was Monday, and I had to go with Dad to the station to catch a train to take me to boarding school, a hundred miles away.

We lived in such a remote part of South Africa that the nearest girls' school of my parents' choice was more than a hundred miles away, so we had to become boarders at the school.

Still half asleep, I got dressed as fast as I could while my mom went to make hot cocoa and wrap up some sandwiches she made for me the night before. That would be my breakfast on the train. Because the train stopped at each siding along the way, the journey always took at least six to seven hours. It felt like *forever*.

As soon as I was dressed, Dad would load my suitcases into the car; Mom would give us the cocoa and sandwiches, kiss me goodbye, and we would leave. The station was about five miles from our farm on a dirt road. The cocoa was for us to sip and keep warm while we waited for the train. We had to get there long before the train was due to arrive at the station. I was the only one catching it, so we had to make sure we got there on time just in case it arrived early as it would not wait for us. It would barely stop long enough for me to jump on. I had caught the train with my eldest sister for my first two years, but when she graduated from high school, I had to catch the train alone. I hated that.

I can remember so vividly sitting there in the car in the very quiet pitch darkness of the African night. There were no lights from the town to lighten the sky. All we could see were millions of stars, sparkling like diamonds in that pitch-black sky.

Dad and I used to sit there, me bundled in blankets, sipping the hot cocoa. The only sounds we heard on those dark nights were very loud crickets. Occasionally, far away in the distance, we would hear a jackal crying out. I always worried that the jackal might be catching baby lambs. I remember sitting there for what sometimes felt like ages waiting for the train.

I hated going to boarding school, and I would always hope that we had the wrong night, the train would not arrive, or the conductor would forget about me and forget to stop the train. But the train always came, and it always stopped. We would hear it first in the quiet night and then see its bright lights coming around the corner, piercing the blackness.

As soon as we heard the screechy brakes, my dad would get my suitcases out of the trunk, and we would hurry up onto the platform, looking for the conductor's flashlight. He would be standing at the door closest to my compartment, waving his flashlight to show us where I needed to get on.

My dad would give me a quick kiss and hug and hand the conductor my cases. The conductor would then take my hand to help me up. After he flashed his light at the engine driver, the train would start moving immediately, often barely before I had time to get on.

The conductor would then show me to my compartment and make up my bed. Sometimes I would be in a compartment with five older women, and I hated that. I was desperately shy and always felt so uncomfortable.

Other times, I would be alone in a three-bunk compartment. I liked that, even though I was terrified to be alone. I was always afraid that the conductor would come back because he had a key to my compartment. The train was so noisy; who would hear if I screamed? It was still better being alone than with five strangers, however.

As soon as the conductor closed my compartment door, I would lock it and wedge my suitcases up under the door handle so no one could get in. No one ever did, and the conductor never came and worried me. I was always safe. God was always there protecting me! "He will cover you with his feathers, and under his wings you will find refuge; his faithfulness will be your shield and rampart." (Psalm 91:4 NIV) "Be strong and courageous. Do not be afraid or terrified because of them, for the Lord your God goes with you; he will never leave you nor forsake you." (Deuteronomy 31: 6. NIV)

The train stopped at every siding along the way. There were many stops, and I hardly ever slept those six to seven hours. They felt like forever. I would lie on the bunk, waiting for the sun to come up. At least I was able to look at the scenery outside. It helped pass the time.

We all lived in a hostel near our school run by a lady and her husband, Mr. and Mrs. Johnson. She was so mean, and he was *very* creepy. I always hoped that Mrs. Johnson would be at the station to pick me up, but Mr. Johnson usually came. I would rather have put up with her silent treatment than his creepiness!

Once we got to the hostel, I would quickly unpack my clothes, wash my face, and walk to school. Mr. Johnson sometimes offered me a ride to school, but the ride from the station was more than enough, and I was happy walking to school because it would take longer than a ride in the car, which meant less time in class that first day.

In the beginning, I got *very* homesick. We could not call home because there were no public phones at the hostel. If we really needed to call home in an emergency, we had to ask Mrs. Johnson to call for us. It cost a lot, and we were too scared to ask her. And anyway, we all knew she would sit and listen to our calls. I never called home in those two years at that horrible place.

My mom wrote a long letter to me every week, which would be waiting for me when we got back from school every Tuesday. I remember taking my letters outside where no one could see me reading them because I cried every time I read and re-read her letters, and I did not want any of the girls to see me crying. Later on, when I got used to boarding school, I could read my mom's letters without crying. I guess I got used to being away from home and became less homesick.

At first, boarding school was really hard. There were about fifty of us girls at the hostel, and even though we made wonderful, lifelong friends, it was so hard being away from my parents, and especially growing up without my mom—not being able to talk to her or get help when I was struggling. A couple of the girls were really mean, and I had no one to talk to about this. I wrote to my parents each week, but I could never write about my struggles in the letters, so I just kept quiet and learned to bottle it up.

We went home by train four times a year for our school holidays, which was wonderful, but it meant going back to school at the end of the holidays and catching the train at two o'clock in the morning. But at least I got to see my family on the farm.

Jane, my eldest sister, was at school in Queenstown as well, but she was in a different boarding hostel and at the high school, so I rarely saw her, nor could I call her. I did see her at school during my first year in high school, though.

Afternoons were like at any other school. We had practice for team tennis in summer and field hockey in winter. After practice, we would go back to the hostel for an hour's homework, supper, and then another two hours of homework before bed.

Mrs. Johnson was strict during homework. We were not allowed to talk to anyone. If we had a question, we had to put up our hands and wait for her to come and help us. She was so mean that we actually preferred Mr. Johnson taking us for homework because he was less strict and getting a little deaf, so we could whisper to each other without getting into trouble. He was, as I said, very creepy, but she was a cold, nasty person.

I remember getting very sick when I was at the hostel. I was feeling *horrible* and asked her if I could stay home from school. She felt my forehead with the back of her hand and told me to go to school because I was "pretending to be sick." How I got through school that day, I will never know. I was so sick. That evening, I was worse, but she made me sit through three hours of homework. Fortunately, Mr. Johnson took us for homework that night, and I slept the entire three hours with my head on my hands.

The next day, I was so sick I could hardly get myself to the bathroom. She eventually took me to the doctor, but by then, I had a fever of 105 and was immediately admitted to hospital with pneumonia. I spent ten days in hospital. My mom was furious when she heard what had gone on and that Mrs. Johnson had not called to tell her I was sick until I was admitted into hospital.

High school was much better. I went to live in another hostel near the high school. A lot of my friends came to the same hostel, which was great. Catching the train to school had also gotten a lot easier and less frightening, I was so used to it by now, but I still hated it. On a couple of occasions, a friend who lived about thirty-five miles from our farm caught the train to school with me. It was great having company.

I loved sport at high school and played team tennis and field hockey. Boarding school was much easier now, and I had made many friends—very special ones because we all understood how hard it was growing up away from our parents. We formed special bonds between each other, and a lot of us have remained friends for life.

After school, I went to nursing college in Cape Town. While working in Cape Town, I decided to come and travel around America and planned on working here for a year.

Before I left for the United States, I went to visit my parents, who had since retired from the farm to a retirement village at the coast. I was sitting with my mom on her bed one of those mornings. She was doing some sewing, and I was sitting chatting with her, drinking some tea. We somehow got onto the subject of boarding school and trains.

"I *loathed* catching the train," I told her.

"I know," she responded.

"You knew?" I asked, surprised.

"Yes," she said.

"Why didn't you say something to me, Mom? I think it would have helped me. I was too scared to say something to you."

"My darling, what could I say? I did not like putting you on that train so young, but we had no other option. We had the school boarders with us during the week and couldn't leave them."

She had started a public school on our farm. Initially it had been so she could keep my siblings and me at home and homeschool us and not have to send us to town to become weekly boarders. Later, when she was told she could no longer homeschool us, she applied to the school board and was granted a license to open up a government farm school.

"Mom, I always felt that you didn't love me or care about me," I told her. I'm sure it hurt her a lot, but it was the truth.

"Of *course,* I loved you!" she said. "It was just the way we did things then. We had to be strong. I did the same when I went to boarding school. I had to be strong."

"I understand, Mom, but I know it would have helped me cope better. I still hate trains to this day!" It makes so much sense now. Our parents' generation was a lot more stoic than our generation. You just did it without complaining. It was just like that in those days. One did what needed to be done and never questioned it.

I think I was just a very sensitive child and lacked confidence. I was teased a lot at school, and sometimes, the girls were nasty, and I think I carried a lot of pain due to it. I also took a lot of it to heart, never showing it, always laughing. I believe this gave them permission to continue because I could not stick up for myself. But being sensitive, it hurt me, and that obviously did not help my confidence and low self-esteem.

On that same trip, I went back to the farm where I grew up to spend a few days with my brother Steve, sister-in-law Doreen, and my niece and nephew Charles and Carolanne to say goodbye.

It was wonderful going back to the farm, and being there brought back many childhood memories. I especially enjoyed spending time with Carolanne and Charles, who were six and four years old, respectively.

On the Sunday night, two days before I was to leave for Johannesburg prior to flying to America, Doreen put the two children to bed—Charles first, being the youngest.

Then it was time for Carolanne to go to bed. Monday morning meant getting up to go to school for her. Steve and Doreen had decided to send her as a weekly boarder to the local school thirty-five miles away from the farm. She was not as lucky as we had been, having our mom teach us on the farm until we were eleven years old.

I kissed her good night and told her I would see her when I came back from America. The darling little girl hugged me so tightly, it made my eyes well up with tears.

About fifteen minutes after Doreen had turned off her light, she called her mom. Doreen got up to go and see what she wanted.

"What did she want?" I asked Doreen when she came back.

"She says she's cold," Doreen replied. "I don't know why. She has plenty of blankets. I gave her another one anyway."

About fifteen minutes later, Carolanne called her again. I could hear her crying. Doreen got up and went to her room. I heard her telling Carolanne that she *couldn't* be cold. She had five blankets on her bed. I also heard her telling her that she had to go to sleep because she had school the next day.

Suddenly, I froze. It felt as if time had stopped. My thoughts went back twenty years. That was *me* in that bed. I could just see myself the night before I was due to catch that train to go to boarding school. I remembered it so vividly, how sad I had felt and how much I had dreaded going to bed on those nights. I wanted to cry for her.

The third time she called for her mom, Doreen was irritated. "What on earth is wrong with that child! She *can't* still be cold!"

"I'll go and see what she wants," I said, getting up quickly and going to her room. Sitting down on the side of her bed, I asked her if I could hold her hand.

"Yes." A little squeak came from the mountain of blankets between the sobs. Tears welled up in my eyes. *Thank goodness its dark,* I thought.

I sat there for a while, trying to compose myself. When I could speak, I told her that when I was a little girl, I also went to boarding school and had to catch the train in the middle of the night and that my dad, her Poppah, would take me up to the station to catch the train. I told her that I used to get *very* sad on Sunday nights when bedtime came. It meant catching the train and going away to school the next day. But, I said, even though it was horrible going to school, I had made many wonderful friends and was still friendly with them, even now that I was older. "You have made some very special friends at school, haven't you?" I asked, trying to distract her.

"Yes." She had stopped crying and was listening to me.

"Mom tells me you love tennis and are really good. It is fun playing tennis with our friends, isn't it?"

"Yes." A quiet little whisper from the bed. Taking in another deep breath and still trying to compose myself, I told her that I loved playing tennis too.

"I know it is very hard to leave Mom, Dad, and Charles on Monday morning to spend the week at boarding school, but you have lots of friends, and, of course, your tennis. And Mom tells me you are doing very well at your schoolwork." I paused a while, waiting for her to take it all in. "Now, I want you to promise me something. Promise me that you will remember this *forever*. We love you *so* much! Your mom, dad, and Charles miss you so much when you are at school.

They can't *wait* for Friday because you come home on Friday. And, you only have four more sleeps, and you will be back home!" I paused again. "Will you remember that for me?"

"Yes," she said, her voice sounding a little stronger now. She had also stopped crying. I bent over and hugged her tightly, pausing for a while at the bottom of her bed.

"Okay, I am going to let you sleep now." I took off one of the blankets. She wouldn't need it. "Now remember, four more 'sleeps,' and you will be home. And we love you *very* much!" I reminded her.

I'm sure she was asleep before I left her room. I don't think she even heard my last sentence. Tears were running down my cheeks as I walked away. I felt so *sad* for her. She was so young and so little lying in that big bed. Imagine spending weeks away from her parents at that age? I quickly wiped away my tears and composing myself, went back to the family room. I told Doreen I thought she was crying because she was sad since she had to go to school the next day and that I had reassured her that she would be home in four "sleeps." I hoped Doreen would remember that the following Sunday night and remind her.

Thirteen years later, I was living in California. Carolanne had excelled in tennis at school and was here in America on a four-year tennis scholarship at McNeese State University in Louisiana. She had come to spend her Christmas break with us. She was nineteen years old.

As the afternoon turned into evening on the first Sunday she was here, I noticed her getting quieter and looking somewhat pensive.

"Are you alright?" I asked her.

"Yes," she answered.

But I could feel that there was something bugging her and that she was possibly holding something back. Sensing that there was more to it than she was admitting but not wanting to pry too much, I went on telling her that after leaving boarding school, I never liked Sunday evenings. I always felt a little flat, even after all these years.

"We used to call it our Sunday night/Monday morning blues," I told her.

"We did too!" Suddenly, my mind went back to the last time I had seen her, on the farm, a little girl crying in her bed, not wanting to go to boarding school the next day. My heart sunk.

"You won't remember, but when you were six, I came to the farm to say goodbye to you before coming to America. My last night there was a Sunday night. You had gone to bed and were crying. You told your mom that you were cold. But I believed that you were sad because you had to go to school the next day. I made you promise me..." but I never completed my sentence. She had put her hand up to stop me talking, her beautiful blue eyes filling with tears.

"I have never forgotten that night. You told me four more sleeps, and I would be home!" By then, *I* had tears rolling down my cheeks. How amazing. I had forgotten about it, suppressed the memory, I'm sure, because it made me so sad until we were talking about the "Sunday night blues" that afternoon, thirteen years later.

Looking back now, I like to think that I helped that sad little girl lying in her bed on that Sunday night thirteen years prior. I hope so because she never forgot my advice to her. Going to boarding school by train was very hard for me. But God never gives us more than we can handle. Even though we sometimes feel circumstances are more than we can cope with, He is with us all the time. He protected me on every trip. And I believe in retrospect that the whole experience strengthened me.

I think, I hope, without arrogance, that it was no coincidence me being on the farm that night. I also believe my experience at school helped me *hear* that little girl's sadness. So often, we listen to people talking. Children talking. But how often do we halt our thoughts and our internal chatter to really *hear* what they are saying?

Doreen did not *hear* what Carolanne was trying to say. I'm sure that all she could think of was that her child had to go to sleep because she had school the next day. And that is so true. As a mom, she knew that she had to go to sleep; otherwise, she would probably fall asleep in class the next day. All mothers would tell their children exactly the same.

However, I believe what she didn't pick up was that the little child was sad, and didn't know how to tell her mommy that she did not want to leave them and spend the week away from them. She wanted to stay on the farm with them. She was trying to tell her mommy but did not know *how* to tell her.

I believe the only way I heard it was because I had been there, in that very bedroom, many years ago, the night before I had to catch the train. I had been sad, and I, too, hadn't been able to tell my mom. I didn't know how to.

Strangely, all of a sudden, all my struggles going to boarding school felt as if they were meant to be. I believe there is always a reason for everything and that God places us in situations or places where we can help others. We can use our experiences, as hurtful as they sometimes are, to help others. When we have walked in their footsteps, we can understand and empathize all the more and feel what that person is going through.

I also believe that it is so important for us to sometimes just listen. If we can learn to turn off the internal "chatter" and hear what someone is saying, listen with our hearts and not our minds, we might just be in a place one day where we can lend a helping hand and make a difference for someone, young or old, who is afraid, sad, and hurting. It may sound simple, but I believe it can be profound. It somehow just feels better when we know someone has really *heard* us.

CHAPTER 2

The Farm Girl from South Africa: My Story

I grew up on a ranch in a very remote part of South Africa. I was one of five children. Not long after my twin brother and I were born, my sister Mary started showing symptoms and was diagnosed with a very rare condition called lipoid proteinosis, also known as Urbach-Wiethe disease. I believe that she was a little over two years old at the time. At the beginning of her illness, it meant trips to doctors for her and my parents. Each doctor's visit meant a trip to a city named Bloemfontein, which was three hours away. They had to drive there because no doctor in our area had heard about her condition and therefore had referred her to specialists in that particular city.

Fortunately, our grandparents lived on the ranch with us, their house only about a couple hundred yards from ours, which was very convenient as they were able to take care of my eldest brother Tom, sister Jane, twin brother Stephen, and me when my parents took my sister for her doctors' visits, which sometimes meant they had to sleep over to see more specialists the next day.

At this time, my grandmother was teaching my eldest brother Tom, and my mom was kept busy with my eldest sister Jane, four years old, Mary two years old, Stephen and me, a few months old. When Steve and I were two years old, my mom took over teaching Tom and had started teaching Jane, then six. Nonini, our nurse maid, helped with Mary, Steve, and me while my mom was homeschooling the other two.

Nonini was the daughter of a couple who were working on the farm, Fanie and Paulina. Paulina was the cook for my grandparents, and Fanie worked on the farm. They were a wonderful, lovable, and loyal family. They lived and worked on our farm for over seventy years.

Nonini was an amazing person. She and her parents were from the Bantu tribe. They spoke Xhosa, an African language. It is often referred to as the "click" language because there are many clicking sounds in it. My mom tried very hard to encourage Nonini to teach all of us children how to speak Xhosa, offering to pay her well, but she was determined to learn English and Afrikaans, both languages of which she spoke fluently anyway. I have always been sorry that she did not teach us kids because I would love to be able to speak Xhosa fluently. It is such a fascinating language!

It is custom for Bantu women to get married at an early age and have a large family. They are often frowned upon and questioned as to what is "wrong" with them if they don't follow tradition. Nonini chose not to follow tradition and never married. She worked for my parents for many years—at first, looking after us children, and then she helped with the weekly boarders when Mom started the government school on the farm. Later, when we all went to boarding school, Mom continued with the farm school, and Nonini stayed on working for her, as well as taking care of both her own parents until they passed away. She continued working for my brother and sister-in-law for a while after my parents retired and moved down to the coast. At a later date, she moved into town and retired. What an amazing Christian lady she was. She was like a second mom to us. More about her later.

When Stephen and I were four years old, my eldest brother Tom, who was ten at the time, was diagnosed with brain cancer. It happened very suddenly. It was June and apparently a bitterly cold winter. Winter nights on the farm were dark. My mom described them best in her book, "The nights are always clear there with usually a magnificent array of stars in the sky."

She wrote that my dad had taken Tom over to my Uncle Jock's house to look at the stars through our great-grandpa's telescope, a very exciting night for Tom. Apparently, they came home at ten o'clock. The rest of us children were already asleep in bed, and Mom was sitting at the fire in the lounge.

As I mentioned earlier on, we had no electricity at the farm and therefore no central heating, so my mom would build a big fire in the lounge in the hearth, and we would sit around in the evenings, reading and playing games. We did have the generator, which Dad started when it got dark in the late evenings and turned it off when he and my mom went to bed. We had lights, just no central heating.

According to my mom, Tom was sitting on the little stool near the fire warming himself after returning from star gazing. I can imagine him telling my mom about the stars and planets they had seen through the telescope. My mom then told him it was time to go to bed. She writes that apparently Tom got up, yawned, stretched, and then looked at my mom and told her he was "seeing double." She put him to bed, and apparently, he slept very well.

The next day, she could see that he did not look well at all, so she called the doctor in town. My dad took him into town to see our family doctor, who immediately detected pressure on his brain. They went home and the next day left very early for Bloemfontein, a city about three hours' drive from the farm. By the time they arrived, Tom could hardly walk. My mom told us he lay on his back and slept the entire way to Bloemfontein.

After many tests, X-rays, and a spinal tap, it was revealed that he had a blockage in his brain, causing the brain fluid to collect and causing a lot of pressure in his brain. Tom was diagnosed with a malignant brain tumor. I can't imagine how shocked my parents must have been. Two days before that, Dad and Tom had been looking at the stars through my great-grandpa's telescope, and now they were in hospital, and he was critically ill with a canccrous brain tumor, and the specialists were not sure he would survive his surgery.

After an eight-hour surgery to remove the tumor, they wheeled Tom out of the operating room. My mom and dad were waiting in the corridor when they brought him out. It was the 19th of July, my mom's birthday, and as she wrote in her book:

> "I was devastated. After his long operation, we were sitting in the corridor waiting for them to bring him back to the ward. Reverend A. J. Western was the minister at Trinity Church, and simultaneously, as the minister walked up to us and put his arm around me, they wheeled Tom back on the gurney. During the operation he had to have a large section of his skull cut out at the back of his head. He had been lying on his face for all those eight hours. His face was so swollen we could hardly recognize him. As he got to us, there was a "warm sensation of wind" that engulfed us. We *all* felt it. In fact, the orderlies commented on the sudden "warm wind." I know it was the Holy Spirit comforting and strengthening us at that dramatic moment. What an amazing comfort."

What an amazingly strong woman my mom was, her faith so incredibly secure.

Mom sat at Tom's bedside from six o'clock in the morning until ten o'clock at night in that hospital for nine weeks. She says the two surgeons visited him every day, never missing a visit.

The four of us children stayed on the farm with my grandparents. Dad would be home during the week to work on the farm and would drive up to spend weekends with Mom and Tom. I don't remember any of that time at all, but I know that Nonini was there every day helping my grandma with us four kids.

After Tom was strong enough to withstand what was then known as "cobalt therapy," which I assume is what we now call radiation, they air-lifted him to Johannesburg to the Princess Nursing Hospital, another three hours from Bloemfontein, a six-hour drive from the farm. I believe my dad and mom followed in the car, and now that they were too far for Dad to drive home during the week, he and Mom stayed up there with Tom.

My parents stayed in Johannesburg for six weeks while Tom had his treatment. Mom actually started helping in the ward this time as he was less critical. She loved helping the nurses with the children and once again stayed with Tom all day. She had always wanted to be a nurse, and I'm sure she found this therapeutic. She got to know all the little children, as well as their parents, and she kept in touch with some of the parents right up to the time she passed away.

Since he could not travel home to be with us, my dad looked for a temporary job in Johannesburg. Once more, my mom wrote: "Through God's Grace, Doug got a job with Robert's Construction, an engineering firm, was occupied and was earning. I was at the hospital all day, every day. The engineer under whom Doug worked, had recently recovered from a brain operation in the Princess Nursing Hospital! Do you see the jigsaw pieces falling into place with God's plan? Incredible." Oh yes, this was no coincidence. I believe it was a God-incidence. It must have given Mom and Dad so much comfort and hope, knowing that the engineer had had brain surgery at the same hospital Tom was in and that he was well and back to work. What an amazing God we have! —also, that Dad was able to get a job with him and earn some money and he would understand if Dad had to go to the hospital when needed.

My dad was a qualified civil engineer and had worked in Rhodesia, now known as Zimbabwe, before they moved back to the farm to live with my grandparents. In fact, Dad designed and built their house in Rhodesia, and he designed and built the house we grew up in on the farm.

One of Dad and Mom's biggest highlights during those long and stressful weeks in Johannesburg was when my Uncle Ed piled my grandma, grandpa, and the four of us children into the car and drove the six-plus hours to go and see them. One cringes when we think that there were no seatbelts those days! But once again, God was there protecting us. My mom wrote about that in her book too. "Edward drove them up to Johannesburg in Dad's car. Quite a squash- three adults and four children! They spent a few days with us. What a tearful reunion and parting!"

After nine weeks in Bloemfontein and another six weeks in Johannesburg, my parents were, as my mom wrote, "At last going home. What joy all around!" She went on to say, "Tom was far from healed, but we took things slowly, and gradually got back to normal."

There were no physio or speech therapists in those days, so Mom had to do it all and still help my grandma, who was teaching Mary and Jane, six and eight years respectively. And, of course, Stephen and I were four. It must have been incredibly hard for everyone, especially my mom. I will say it over and over that she was an amazingly strong lady. I have no doubt that her faith in God got her through. She had such a strong, undeniable faith and believed that it would "all work out according to God's plan." She rarely spoke about this as we were growing up, just believed in God's faithfulness.

She went on to say; "What a joy to be home after three and a half difficult months, and have all my precious children under our roof once more. School resumed, and Tom started bit by bit. What an incredibly brave lad. He had not once questioned his circumstances, and never complained. I believe he 'touched' more people for God than I ever will." Not true, Mom—you have touched *countless* people in your life. Of that, I have no doubt.

"Life on the farm went on quietly, and Tom got stronger," she continued. When he was in sixth grade, they started looking at boarding school for him. They applied to a school that my great-grandfather, who had been a Methodist minister, had co-founded. She wrote that she and dad felt his school life should be as "normal as possible."

They took him to the school and met with the chaplain, telling him Tom's whole story and hoping that he would take a special interest in and help support Tom, being all that he had overcome having been so desperately ill for so long. Apparently, they were horribly disappointed. According to my mom, the chaplain was not at all interested. She has told me before that it was the hardest thing she had ever done. My dad's sister and husband were living in the same city, and my aunt did help Tom when she could, but their lives were busy too.

My mom says that Tom *never* complained, but that she knew he had a hard time and that there was one "fellow who bullied him mercilessly." She did not find this out until much later, and so they took him out of school after eleventh grade and brought him to the farm so he could help Dad. My grandpa was getting older and handing most of the work over to Dad, who needed the help anyway.

I know that my mom struggled with the fact that Tom had been bullied for many years, and she felt a lot of guilt about it, but how was she to know this since Tom never said a word about it? He was so stoic and so brave right from the age of ten when he was diagnosed with brain cancer, throughout his boarding school days, and on the farm until the cancer re-occurred when he was twenty-five years old. I know that my mom's faith in God helped her hand it all over to Him and find comfort and release from her guilt.

Soon after Tom went to boarding school, the school hostel in our local small town was not full enough, and they refused to give Mom the yearly permission to teach us on the farm as she had been doing. They told her that she needed to send the four of us to school to become weekly boarders to help them with their numbers. Mom was not prepared to send us. She felt that were too young to become weekly boarders, and she felt that we were being given a more "holistic" education being home-schooled. (My mom was a qualified teacher.)

She applied to the education department, and the farm became a registered farm school. Three children from neighboring farms joined the school as weekly boarders almost immediately, and as my mom said, "Now we had a real school!"

As the years passed, other children from neighboring farms also joined the school, and at times, there were twelve weekly boarders, making for full bedrooms! Luckily, when Dad had built our house, he had made large bedrooms, and they were easily converted into little dormitories by just adding beds. She used to joke about us being like little sardines in a can!

As my mom said, she never had more than twelve children staying with us, but she also had two who were day scholars, and she was the only teacher, teaching children from first grade to fourth grade alone! It really became a twenty-four-hour job. How she coped, I'll never know.

Around this time, my precious grandmother died very suddenly from a massive stroke. Now Mom had to run two houses as well. She did have Nonini helping with the children, and she did have a cook and housekeeper but no aides in the school and sometimes up to fourteen children to teach. What a strong and amazing mom we had!

As she has said many a time, those fourteen years were incredibly busy years. She had the school farm and my three eldest siblings now at boarding school. She played the organ for church each Sunday, often in different little towns some thirty miles apart, and sometimes in two venues on the same day! She also wrote letters to my siblings every Sunday afternoon. I have often wondered how she did it.

"No-one goes through life without problems and challenges, but those who know and love the Lord can handle the problems in His strength and Grace. Nothing is going to happen today which God and I together, cannot handle," she wrote. And that is exactly how she lived her life—committed to God, never questioning Him, her faith never wavering, serving Him her entire life.

When Stephen and I were eight years old, he sprained his ankle while we were playing tennis. To keep him from using his foot, Mom told him to sit on our tricycle, and two of the school children pushed him around.

One afternoon, my mom was busy in her bedroom on her sewing machine. The rest of us children were playing on the lawn. She wrote that suddenly she heard an agonizing scream. She jumped up and ran outside. The tricycle had toppled sideways on the grass, and Stephen had fallen onto his left hip. He was in a lot of pain. I remember he was white as a sheet. I don't remember who helped her carry him to the lounge. My dad took him straight to town to the hospital to see the doctor and for X-ray's.

My dad told us at a later date that when they drove into town, Stephen, lying on his side on the back seat, pale from all the pain, asked my dad to please fix his hair because he didn't want the doctor to see him with untidy hair! Such a brave child! X-rays revealed a fracture of his femur. My dad had to leave him in the hospital that night and come home.

The next day, my dad went into town and picked him up, taking him to East London, a city about six hours away, so that he could be seen by a pediatric orthopedic surgeon. There were no pediatric doctors in our small town. My mom had to stay on the farm with the school children. It must have been so hard for her, not being able to go with her child.

The next day, he had surgery to repair the fracture, as well as a bone graft because the head of his femur was hollow and had never "filled in," my mom told us. "He had to be on crutches for six weeks, and was amazing. Never once did he complain, and never once did he touch his toes on the ground," my mom wrote in her book. (I do remember us having races, him on his crutches. My mom would have had a fit had she seen us! Typical kids!)

Unfortunately, at his six-week checkup, they discovered that the graft had not taken, and he had to endure another six-hour surgery, with a bone graft taken from his other hip as well as a large pin put into his femur, with a plate and I believe eight screws to stabilize his hip. As I said, he was eight years old at that time, and when I asked him if he had pain, he never said a thing about pain in his leg, but he did say that the "place where they took the bone" hurt him. What an amazing child!

He stayed in hospital on bedrest for two weeks. How different it was in those days. My dad stayed down in East

London with him, and my mom stayed on the farm teaching and taking care of the school children, Mary, and me.

Every night, for those two weeks, she would put the children to bed and then sit down and write Stephen a letter. She would also draw and color a beautiful sketch of one of the *Dennis the Menace* cartoons for Stephen. *Dennis the Menace* was his favorite cartoon. I can't imagine how tired my mom was at the end of each day, and yet she unselfishly sat down and drew and colored Stephen a cartoon, wrote a letter, prepared classes for the next day, and only then did she go to bed—every night for the two weeks he was in hospital. The love and unselfish devotion of a mother is truly amazing. When my dad brought Stephen back, my mom wrote that life on the farm and at the school went on once more as usual.

She had also applied to the board of education to start a school for the little black children on our farm and the surrounding farms. Because of the horrific apartheid, they were obviously not allowed to attend our school, but Mom wanted them to have the same education we were getting, so she interviewed and installed a teacher for them. They built a school house for the children and a home for the teacher.

My last year on the farm was a lonely one for me. My twin Stephen had decided he wanted to go to boarding school a year earlier because he loved cricket and wanted to go to "big" school and play there. I stayed home for that year, but the school children were a lot younger than I was, and it was not the same without him. Weekends were lonely too. The children were weekly boarders, so I was alone, except for the odd weekend that Mary came home from boarding school. I'm sure it was just a bit of separation anxiety without my twin brother, but it was a hard year for me. I did discover a love of reading and became an avid reader and still am today, but it just wasn't the same without him.

Mom had the farm school for fourteen years. She earned very little, really, especially for the amount of work it entailed, but it was enough to help get us through high school, and all five of us got a very good education thanks to her with the school and Dad's hard work on the farm.

I went off to boarding school after grade six and then down to Cape Town to nursing school after I graduated from high school.

CHAPTER 3

Never Let Anyone Dim Your Light

I stood in front of the elevator door, impatiently waiting for it to arrive on my floor so that I could take it down to the long underground tunnel and from there, up and into the hospital—my crisp, white uniform perfectly starched and ironed; my nurse's cap securely pinned into my hair, which was, in turn, brushed back and held securely in a high, tight ponytail; not a stray hair out of place. It was my first month in nursing school, and I did not want to be late for duty.

Finally, the elevator arrived on my floor. I stepped in and firmly pressed the "tunnel" button. The doors closed slowly, and the elevator started descending. *Ping*, it went as it passed the laundry. *Who on earth would put a huge laundry facility underground? Imagine working there like a mole, all day and night. How awful!* I thought. *It is always so hot and humid in there.* Gladly some people did, hence my perfectly starched, pristine white uniform.

The next floor down was the entryway to the tunnel that went to the morgue, or so we had been told. It had only opened once when a group of us junior nurses were in the elevator, and we all held our breaths as the doors opened. All we saw was a dark, green, gloomy, eerie tunnel leading away. Someone closest to the buttons banged on them, hoping it would close quickly and we would descend before we saw a creepy gurney with a covered body wheeled by. There was a collective sigh of relief from us all when the doors closed and the elevator descended to the main tunnel leading to the hospital.

Ping, the elevator sounded as it went past the floor to the morgue. I was alone in the elevator this time, and I let out a huge sigh of relief. I did not want it to stop and the doors to open with me alone in the elevator. I was so relieved when the elevator stopped at the tunnel and I could get out and walk quickly down the long tunnel to the elevator that would take me up to the fifth-floor pediatric ward, where I had just started my first three-month rotation. I loved little children and found it rather coincidental, since I hadn't ever wanted to become a nurse, that my first three months' training would be in the pediatric ward.

As a child and long into adulthood, I struggled a lot with very low self-esteem and low self-confidence. I was also an extremely sensitive person. Critical and harsh words would literally cut right through me, and I would immediately blame myself for being ugly, stupid, fat, unworthy, or any other self-deprecating adjective I could think of when I was being teased in a mean way or when someone was running me down. I have often thought that people also treated me the way I treated myself, and I was often teased and made fun of.

I learned to laugh at myself at a young age, which can be good, but it also gave others permission to tease me. By just laughing it off, I believe that people did not realize how much their words hurt me, and because I always laughed regardless of how mean the teasing was, I gave them permission to continue teasing me. I did not have the confidence to stop them. It was almost a vicious cycle. At times, later on in my career, I would be teased so much that I would leave work in tears. I'm talking about nasty, disparaging teasing. I will explain what I mean by this later on in the book.

I have often wondered if leaving home at the age of eleven to attend boarding school had a lot to do with my low self-confidence. Not having my parents around me for months on end was so hard. I didn't have a parent figure to help me or talk to when others hurt me. I just absorbed it into my subconscious and laughed. Even when sad and hurt, I would just laugh. I know there are thousands of children who go to boarding school and manage very well. I think I was just a more sensitive child. I will add, though, that laughter can be wonderfully therapeutic, and I laugh a lot even to this day!

Toward the middle of my final year in high school, I had to start thinking about my future, as all high schoolers do. What was I going to do after school? I had not ever really felt a calling to do anything. Maybe because of my lack of self-confidence? I knew that I loved children, animals, birds, and nature, but in those days, we really had three choices—become a secretary, a nurse, or a teacher. I had no desire to become a secretary or a nurse. Therefore, knowing that I loved children, I started thinking about becoming a preschool teacher.

I remember talking with my mom during our three-week July school vacation when I was home on the farm. She was becoming concerned because I had not made up my mind, and we had to start applying to colleges before they filled up.

By the end of my three-week vacation, I applied to two teachers' training colleges—one in Cape Town and one in Grahamstown, a city closer to the farm. Both colleges happened to have "waiting" lists, and the one with the shortest waiting list was in Cape Town. The college told us it was an eighteen-month waiting list. I had no idea what I would do while I waited. There were no jobs locally in our small town, and anyway, it was too far to drive there and back each day.

It was then that my mother suggested that I apply to nursing school. She thought it would be a great way to see if I would enjoy nursing, and if not, I could stop nursing and go to the teachers' training college when an opening became available.

I discovered years later that my mom, who had been a teacher all her life, had actually wanted to become a nurse, but her parents had encouraged her to become a teacher instead. It made sense to me that she was absolutely delighted when I was accepted into nursing school!

I was accepted at nursing school in Cape Town, starting date set for March 1st, twenty days before my eighteenth birthday. We packed my bags, and I headed off to Cape Town, about a thousand miles away from home.

It was really frightening starting nursing school so far from home, especially knowing that we only got one month off a year. That meant only seeing my parents once a year after having been used to going home four times a year when I was at boarding school. At least I would be able to call home from Cape Town.

I lived in the nurses' residence for the first year and a half. The school expected us to live in the residence for the first year. I think it was a good idea because all the other first-year nurses stayed in "Res," as we called it, and I met a lot of nurses and made a lot of very special friends. I am still close to many of them to this day.

I did not like nursing. I happen to be very queasy, a germaphobe, and have a very keen sense of smell, which does not help if one is queasy! I hated seeing people in pain, sick, and suffering, and we worked on the floors throughout our entire training, going to college for a few months here and there. It was a very thorough training. We worked very hard and were exposed to a lot of pain, suffering, and sadness.

Although I did not like nursing, I made a promise to myself at the very beginning I would never ever let my patients know or sense that I did not want to be a nurse. I promised myself that I would always treat every patient the way I would want to be treated or the way I would want my family treated. Because of this, I was extremely conscientious and worked and studied extremely hard. My grades were good, and my parents were delighted.

Toward the end of my second year, with one year to go before I graduated, my mom called me to say that they had received a letter for me from the teachers' training college saying that I had been accepted to the school. Now came the decision; should I leave nursing and go to TC, as we called it, or should I spend one more year at the hospital and become a qualified registered nurse? Of course, my parents suggested that I finish nursing school, telling me that I would always be able to fall back on it should I not enjoy teaching, and, "Why waste all your nursing training?" they said. That advice proved to be very useful most of my life.

It did make a lot of sense, but it was still a difficult decision for me to make. I really wanted to leave nursing. However, for the first time in my life, I had felt completely validated by my parents. So, I stayed on and never went on to teach.

I learned a lot about myself at nursing school. I learned during those years that I was a very sensitive person. People walked all over me, and I allowed them to do so. But I also learned that I was a compassionate and caring person, and consequently, my patients loved me. That gave me strength to continue. And because my patients loved me, I think the doctors gained a new respect for me.

Having developed a very strong sense of humor at boarding school helped a lot, too. I laughed a lot with my patients and also with the doctors and staff. I was told that I had a "sunny disposition" and was nicknamed "Sunshine" by many of the staff. Initially, that helped build my self-confidence. However, when some of the other nurses saw the respect I got from the doctors, some of them became very nasty, and being very sensitive, that nearly destroyed me.

Being so passionate about my patients helped me get through nursing school and has helped me all these years. But it took a toll on my confidence, and after been bullied for years and years, I lost every bit of self-confidence I had worked so hard to build. But I still laughed a *lot* because I found that it relieved my stress and definitely helped me cope. A double-edged sword, that's for sure.

I came to the US thirty years ago and started working at a hospital in Los Angeles. I initially came to travel around the United States, see all the states, play golf, and then return to South Africa. I also came, I think subconsciously, to escape some very toxic relationships in South Africa. I had been through a very tough time there and needed to get away.

I was lucky enough to have a job to come to, but it was still tough arriving in a foreign country alone with two suitcases and $1,000. But there were eleven other nurses who came over a month after I did, and that helped a lot.

I settled down fairly quickly. I'm sure that having left home to go to boarding school at the age of eleven helped too. There is always a good lesson to be learned in every tough situation.

I was still living in Southern California when I met and married my husband. It was my first marriage. He had two daughters, thirteen and seventeen years old, when we got married. They had lost their mom to cancer. I got married, moved sixty-five miles from my home, and started a new job within a few months. Talk about taking on a lot at one time! It was the hardest thing I have ever done. It was also very hard for my husband and two teenage daughters, I know. I sometimes wondered how and if we would get through it all.

Worst of all was my situation at work. Once more, I got on very well with most of my coworkers and the doctors, but the director of nursing and a couple of her friends took an instant disliking to me and bullied me for the eleven years I was there. I felt trapped there and once more lost all the self-confidence I had fought so hard to build.

I turned once again to eating and put on a *lot* of weight, which certainly did not help my situation, and I felt ashamed and disgusted with myself. During this time, I decided that I wanted to get out of traditional nursing for good and enrolled myself in a class at a nearby college to get my degree in health administration, thinking that I would be able to find a better job locally and get away from my toxic director of nursing, some of the staff, and demeaning doctors. This meant more work and many hours of study, but I figured it would be worth it in the long run.

One Saturday night, my husband and I went to a party at the home of some longtime friends of his. I only knew the host and one other couple at the party. As we arrived, I saw the one couple we knew sitting at a table, which had two empty seats next to them. I immediately asked them if we could join them. They said yes, and feeling very relieved, I sat down. My husband went to get drinks for us.

We chatted for a short while about the girls, their kids, and then they asked me how college was going. I said very well. I noticed a couple sitting across the table from me. I could see that they were very well-dressed and looked very professional and wealthy. The lady immediately asked me what college I was attending.

"University of Laverne," I told her.

"Oh," she responded. "University of Laverne. If you *ever* go to the East Coast and someone asks you where you got your degree, they will have absolutely *no idea* where that college is or how good your education was. I am an attorney, and *I* graduated from an Ivy League college. *Everyone* will know that I received an Ivy League education."

I was totally taken aback. Wow, I thought, what's wrong with her? I've never even seen her before. She seems almost angry the way she responded to me! Having nothing to say, I just smiled.

She then asked me where I came from and where my accent was from. I told her South Africa.

"Oh, that's where the British sent their *convicts!*" she said, a lot louder, and with the same deprecating tone of voice. I could almost *feel* the distaste in her voice.

"Well, actually, that was Australia," I told her. "The British and Dutch settled in South Africa so they had a station to stop and get fresh fruit, vegetables, and meat en route to India so they would not get scurvy."

I'm not sure if it angered her that I had corrected her or if she was embarrassed that I had pointed out her error, but she continued to almost attack me with her words.

"Do the British look down on you South Africans? Do they treat you like *second-class* citizens when you go to England?" she asked in the same tone of voice. I was shocked.

"Well, actually no, the South Africans and British get along very well. There are thousands of South Africans living and working in Britain and thousands of British people living and working in South Africa," I told her.

By now, everyone at the table had stopped talking and was listening to her unsolicited onslaught. I felt as if everyone was watching me. There was a palpable, tense, uncomfortable silence at the table, except for her barrage of questions. I was so embarrassed and devastated and felt close to tears. I could not understand where this had come from. I had never met her nor *seen* her before. Why would a stranger almost attack me verbally when meeting me for the first time? I could not understand it and was embarrassed and flabbergasted.

By the time my husband got back to our table, she had turned to her husband and was talking to him, never glancing my way for the rest of the evening. I was so relieved but felt so uncomfortable and couldn't *wait* to go home. I really don't remember a thing about the rest of the evening. I don't think I said another word for the night and did not tell my husband about her onslaught for many years. I was too embarrassed. I know I was afraid that he might start seeing me as a "second class citizen." Of course he would never be like that, but my self-esteem was really low after that.

After that evening, I once again retreated into my shell. I felt defeated, demoralized, and very alone. How would I go out and use my degree if that's what people thought of South Africans? What would be the use of spending all that money to get a degree and not be able to use it? I went into a very dark place for a long time. I dropped my classes, and as I had done many a time in my life, I turned to food for comfort, putting on even more weight. That made it all so much worse—back to self-loathing, hating my weakness and the fact that I could not stand up for myself; wondering why I allowed people to bully and belittle me, run me down and walk all over me, and why I did not have the confidence to stop them, stand up to them, and walk away. I wondered what was wrong with me.

And the sad thing is that I, and only I, allowed that insecure lady attorney to make me feel inferior and halt my dreams for *years*. I have no doubt that she never gave me another thought, and yet I allowed her to make me feel inferior, stupid, and incompetent and give up my dreams of getting my university degree.

It was a good lesson for me, a tough one that took a long time to learn. Strangely, I think it strengthened me and made me stronger. We *can* recover from hurt and use it to make us stronger.

Looking back, I know without a doubt that being able to laugh helped me through all those difficult years.

Laughter heals. It lifts me up. Even at my lowest times, I have laughed a lot. Laughter also draws people to you.

A friend once told me: "You are not letting God's light shine through you." After thinking about that for a very long time, I started to believe that God had given me the gift of laughter and a light to shine. I believe that is why some of the doctors and some of my friends still call me "Sunshine," and why a director of nursing during my first few years told me I had a "sunny disposition."

I am working on myself all the time and I pray that no one will dim that light again or, more importantly, that I will never *allow* anyone to dim that light again. God gives us *all* a light to shine. My hope is that you will go out and use yours to make a difference in this world. Sometimes, what seems hardest for us to overcome becomes our message of hope for others.

I pray that you will never let anyone dim your light.

CHAPTER 4

My Fears and Insecurities

As a child, I was very sensitive and somewhat insecure. Some of my biggest fears in life were feelings of being unworthy, less than, inferior, and ugly, and at times, I almost obsessed about what people thought about me. I still struggle with many of those feelings today as an adult.

At boarding school, I was lucky enough to have a lot of wonderful friends, but there were a couple of jealous bullies, one being a good friend of mine who suddenly started bullying me. Because I was scared of standing up to their bullying and because at an early age I started laughing a lot, I'm sure as a coping mechanism, I have often wondered if it encouraged them to continue.

On one occasion, I felt brave, and asked one of the bullies to stop calling me by my nickname "Blossom." She just laughed meanly and continued. I stopped asking after that. Being away from my mom, I felt that I had no one to turn to, so I pretended that it did not bug me, but it hurt me a lot.

Our principal knew my mom very well. They had been to school together, and my mom always told me that the principal hated her because my mom had beaten her in tennis in their final year. Apparently, she was furious. She was extremely competitive and lived for her tennis, and when my mom beat her and won *the* coveted trophy, she was devastated. Consequently, when she became the principal during my high school years, she seemed to take an *instant* disliking to me. She never had a nice thing to say to me and on occasion would make some very derisive comments to me in front of my peers, pretending to "tease me" and be funny. But I knew better, and it was extremely hurtful.

The worst time was when we were lining up to go into our final exams for high school. We were lined up along the side of the hall, waiting for the teachers to let us in. Anyone knows how stressful it is going in to write your final exams for high school. They were so strict at our school, and we were terrified. Anyway, along came the principal, chatting to all the girls in line, wishing them luck, encouraging them. When she came to me, she looked at me and in a raised and very deprecating voice said, "*Wow, Blossom!* Just *imagine* seeing you here. Fancy *that!*" and moved on. Not a single word of encouragement, nor did she wish me luck for the exams. What kind of principal does that? I was absolutely shocked, embarrassed, and so upset that she could speak to me like that in front of my friends. Oh yes, even our principal was a bully.

After I was married and working as a nurse at a surgery center, some of the staff and doctors teased me so much that at times, it was so exhausting and demoralizing that I wanted to scream. Some of it also turned to mean and derisive teasing and then to bullying. It was devastating. I talk about this later in my book because I feel so strongly about teasing and bullying.

In the previous paragraphs, I mentioned my nickname. As a young girl, a very beloved family member gave me the nickname "Blossom." I really didn't like it, but I was too scared to say anything. The nickname followed me to school, and I hated that, but it had become such a habit that it stuck and followed me through school and my nursing career, and to this day, some of my friends still call me that. I eventually gave up fighting it and just accepted it.

One day, that same beloved family member started calling me "Blossom Fish-face." I was devastated. Being a child, I guess I took it absolutely literally. I think fish have such ugly faces. (No intention to insult our Creator, but I don't think that fish are pretty!) As a child, it meant to me that I was ugly like a fish, and I think because of this, I grew up feeling ugly. I have often wondered if it is why I grew up desperate to be pretty, beautiful.

I have often wondered just *why* a person would call a child a name like that. I don't think that it was done intentionally to be mean, and I don't think the person even realized how a child could interpret it or personalize it, but it was absolutely devastating to me.

The saying, "Sticks and stones may break my bones but words will never hurt me," is so *wrong,* and I really believe that name-calling can be devastating and definitely a form of bullying if the intention is to be mean or demeaning. We have to remember that children think and perceive things literally and be very careful and aware of this when giving children nicknames, even if we don't mean any harm.

I have never been able to stick up for myself, and this allowed the meanness to continue. I have prayed about it over the years, prayed that God would open my eyes as to why I have suffered from low self-esteem and low self-confidence and have never been able to stand up to those bullying me. I have prayed to understand the reasons so I can improve my self-esteem and confidence. I believe that God created us all to be confident, and yet I have suffered from a lack of it my entire my life.

After boarding school, I went to Cape Town to nursing school. Early on in my second year, I met a guy, and we started dating. He was a rugby player and played for a very popular rugby club down the road from the hospital. I fell madly in love with him. He was my first serious boyfriend, and I was smitten! His emotional abuse started early in our relationship. It was so subtle at first that it was the last thing I would have thought of. Any issues we had were always blamed on me. It was always my fault.

He was a very social person, and after matches, we would stay at the club for a few drinks before we went out for dinner, usually in a large group. He would walk around talking to everyone, loved the ladies, and would often leave me alone for ages. It was fine for him to talk to everyone, but yet if I chatted and laughed with people, especially any of the guys, he would be furious. Often, our evenings ended up in arguments with him telling me I was stupid, fat, and ugly. I was too naïve and young to defend myself and to pick up on any insecurities he had or understand his need to demean and belittle me, and little by little, he chipped away and eroded every little vestige of self confidence and self-esteem I had. I started believing that I was the fat, ugly, and stupid person that he constantly told me I was.

I was amazed when he asked me to marry him, and of course, said yes. We were engaged for a number of years, and his jealousy and abuse seemed to worsen each year. Many a time I wanted to break up with him, but by then, the harm had been done, and I don't know if I was scared to be alone or just so broken down that I had no more fight in me, but I stayed in our toxic relationship far too long.

One night after their team had been badly beaten in a match, we were at the club, and all the guys were basically licking their wounds and drinking too much. I was sitting talking with the wives and girlfriends of the other players, and we were all getting concerned that the guys were drinking too much. I wanted to go home and asked if he would take me home. He ignored me. After a while, I told him I wanted his car keys. He was getting too drunk to drive, and I would take myself home, and he could ask one of the guys to give him a ride home. I think that my telling him he was too drunk to drive infuriated him. He grabbed his keys and stormed outside to his car. I followed and told him that I was driving. This infuriated him more, and he told me to get into the car. I don't know why, but I did. It was too far to walk to my home and not safe to walk alone, and I think I was too embarrassed to go back and ask one of the wives to take me home, so I got in.

We had a huge argument in the car. I told him I was sick and tired of his drinking as well as the way he treated me. Fortunately, we got to the house safely, and our argument continued outside for a bit. Then I told him I was going to bed and walked toward my door. He yelled at me and said we were not done with this argument. I told him I refused to argue with him when he was drunk, that he could have killed me driving in his state, and that I would talk to him the next day when he was sober. I guess walking away from him infuriated him even more, and he came up behind me suddenly and kicked me, a very *hard* kick that hit my inner thigh. I lurched forward, grabbing onto a planter to stop myself from falling over, steadied myself, and then ran for the door. I ran inside and quickly locked the door. I sat down and started crying. My inner thigh ached, I could see a large bruise starting to develop from the top of my inner thigh down my inner leg, and I was absolutely devastated. I just sat there and cried. He got straight back into his car and went back to the clubhouse, I assumed.

I lay awake all night. Thoughts of what had happened to other women in abusive relationships flooded my mind, and I did not want to wait and see where this would end. That night I made up my mind that it was over. This was the last straw. Years of his emotional abuse had almost destroyed me, and now that it had turned to physical abuse, I wondered if it would escalate. I was devastated and wondered how I would get over five years of emotional abuse, but I knew I had to be strong and get out before it was too late.

It took me years to get over it, and those were really dark years. It took me as long to start picking up the pieces of my fragile self-esteem too. I felt so lost, lonely and broken.

Once again, I turned to food and put on a lot weight. To make matters worse, I was also struggling with my job. I was desperate to leave nursing but did not have the courage to look for anything else.

Eventually, I decided to pull myself together, join a gym, get fit, lose weight, and move on with my life. I met and became friendly with the wife of the guy who owned the gym close to my home. She was a darling, so helpful, supportive, and encouraging. I started losing weight, getting fit, and started feeling so much better. I was definitely growing more confident.

One weekend, I was staying with her when her husband was out of town. We got onto the subject of my job, and I told her I was desperate to get out of nursing. She encouraged me to take a course and get certified as a fitness instructor. It sounded like so much fun. The course seemed so interesting, and they covered many of the subjects I had enjoyed in my nursing training. I applied and was accepted and started the class, which was being held at the University of Cape Town Medical School. It was a very comprehensive class and a lot to learn, but I enjoyed it tremendously, and I know it gave my confidence a boost. I still have my certificate hanging on my wall all these years later.

Our plan was to join my friend and help out at their gym, but in the interim, they sadly lost the baby girl she was carrying and decided to move away from Cape Town.

I joined another gym in Constantia, a beautiful suburb of Cape Town. My goal was to get fit and hopefully get a part-time job there and then one day, possibly open my own gym.

Constantia is a very affluent suburb, but it was close to where I shared a townhouse with my sister and a friend, so it was convenient for me to join the gym there. The very first aerobics class I attended, I was surrounded by the most beautiful, fit ladies in their perfect gym attire, being led by even more beautiful instructors. I immediately felt the odd one out, the proverbial ugly duckling. I had been so excited to possibly venture out and change my career, only to have my hopes dashed. I was crushed. I believed that I was the ugly, stupid, fat girl my ex-boyfriend had told me I was for all those years.

Voices in my head chatted constantly, reminding me that I must be delusional to think that I could get involved in teaching aerobics and eventually open up a gym, that I was just a nurse—ugly, stupid, and fat. Nurses can't do that. All that nasty self-doubt and unworthiness crept back in. I just knew that I would *never* have the confidence to do it. My hopes of moving away from nursing were dashed, and I resigned myself to the fact that although I had loved the course, it was obviously not for me. I also stopped going to the gym.

After that, I felt flat and lost again for many years, so much so that surrounded by some toxic relationships that pulled me down further, I decided that I needed a break. I desperately needed a change. After all, they say that sometimes a change is as good as a holiday.

Please don't misunderstand me. I had many wonderful friends from my school and nursing days, but many had moved on, were married, and had children, and although we still had many wonderful times together, it was time for a change.

About this time, I heard that there was a shortage of nurses in the hospitals in the United States. I started to think that I could go over to the US, work for a year, travel, maybe learn to play golf, which I loved, and then come back home and decide what I wanted to do with the rest of my life.

I moved up to Johannesburg to take the entrance exam that would allow me to come and work in the United States for a year. In the hall where we were to sit for the exam, I met Sue, who told me about a company who was recruiting nurses to the Los Angeles area. I applied to the company. The following year, they flew us to California to take the state board exams. While we were there, we interviewed at a few hospitals and then went back home to await our results and possible job offers.

The following June 1991, I flew over to Los Angeles to start working at a hospital in Culver City, California. Although I did have a job to come to, I arrived with two suitcases and $1,000 in my pocket. It was daunting and terrifying, but my years at boarding school helped me, giving me a little confidence. And here I was, ready for my next adventure.

Coming from a small country like South Africa, we were really afraid that we were going to be years behind the medical system here but were pleasantly surprised. Our training had really been strict and comprehensive, and our new nurse manager, Barbara, was very complimentary about our work, experience, and work ethic and made us feel so welcome. We soon made friends, and I am still very close to Barbara, who is now retired and lives in Playa Del Rey, thirty years later and still friendly with a number of the nurses I met when I first came over, some of whom have gone back to their home countries.

During my two years at the hospital in Culver City, I started working a couple of evenings at Santa Monica Hospital Medical Center in Santa Monica. I loved the staff and got on very well with the doctors. I made some wonderful friends there as well. I also started playing golf with a couple of the techs and doctors I worked with. Our group went out quite a bit, and I really felt accepted. I was happier there than I had been for most of my life—most definitely in nursing, anyway.

In December 1994, I was attending a Christmas dinner party at a doctor friend of mine's house. There I met a longtime friend of hers, Gerrit, who happened to be an avid golfer, and we connected immediately! Early in January, we started dating and got married eighteen months later.

CHAPTER 5

What Happened to Me

I started my new life as a wife and stepmother in a new city in July of 1996. The adjustment from being single all my life to being married and having two teenaged stepdaughters living with us was really hard for me. I know it was hard for them as well. They had lost their mom to breast cancer, which was hard enough for them and my husband.

Initially, we decided that I would remain on at the hospital in Santa Monica for a bit of continuity while I got used to my new family and home, but I soon realized that the commute would be too much, so I started looking for a job closer to home.

The only hospital I found that had a vacancy for nurses was a hospital in the neighboring city. Within a few days, I realized that accepting the position there had been a huge mistake. It was the worst hospital I have ever worked in. Strangely enough, my gut had warned me when I interviewed there and saw the place, but I was desperate to find a job closer to home, so I had accepted the position. It was old, and the equipment was antiquated, but most alarming of all, some of the staff who I had started working with were careless, and the standard of care was very poor. They were definitely not the caring, conscientious nurses and techs I had worked with in Santa Monica, and it was very disappointing. I stayed on there for a few months and, once again, went in search for another job.

Soon after I had started my job search, a friend called and referred me to a medical auditing company. The job entailed auditing patients' charts and removing erroneous charges that had been added onto their bills. I interviewed and was offered the position. I was so excited because it was my way out of the operating room but still in the medical field and still serving patients. In my naivety, two things happened that blindsided me. I had so much to learn about life, I guess. The first was when I told the staff at the hospital about the nature of my new job, I was immediately rejected. I was called a "whistle blower" and worse. I was devastated. Don't we all dispute erroneous and fraudulent charges on our own bills? I was shocked and devastated at how I was immediately ostracized and ignored at work. I couldn't wait to get out of that place.

Well, as it turned out, the auditors in the respective hospitals we went to hated us too. They saw it as we were coming in to *steal* their money, not coming to remove a charge or charges that had been billed erroneously. What happened to patient advocacy and ethical practice? I wondered. The rejection really became too much for me. I know we were not supposed to take it personally, but I'm afraid I did and hated it. It also taught me a valuable lesson. I was starting to realize that it was in my character to take things so personally, even if they had nothing to do with me. I found that very interesting. It was something I needed to start working on within myself.

After a year of working under these conditions, I decided it was enough for me. I needed to change my career path. Since I did not want to go straight back into nursing and into the operating room, I went and sat for my real estate license. I figured I liked working with people so would give it a try. Once again in my naivety, I thought that it would be something new and fun. Instead of working with sick patients all day, I could go out and find homes for people. However, I found it extremely competitive with a lot of jealousy, and once again, I realized that it was not what I was searching for. I first made a goal to sell ten houses so that I would not feel as if I had failed yet again. I accomplished that and left.

I then spent a year working at a medical weight loss clinic. I loved my clients, but when I suggested that we bring on a psychologist or counselor to help the clients with their emotional issues and not only the dieting aspect, I was told by the CEO and CNO (chief nursing officer,) that they made their money on the "return" patients. I was appalled at the lack of integrity and glibness of their admission and left.

After that disappointment, I went back to the operating room. I got a job down the road at a new surgery center, as I mentioned earlier on in the book. This was the place where my boss took an instant disliking to me and bullied me for eleven years. People may wonder why I stayed there if she was that nasty to me, but I was so tired from trying other avenues that I just didn't have the energy to move to yet another place or maybe the confidence to start all over again. I do know that I learned some very valuable personal lessons there.

One of those lessons opened up my eyes to the fact that I had always wondered why I turned to food when I was upset or stressed because we all know it is harmful for us to gain and lose many pounds, and as a nurse, I should have known just how harmful it is to our bodies. And yet, I did it over and over again.

I learned the answer one day when a couple of doctors were really nasty and demeaning to me about my weight in front of the staff. I went straight home, and instead of going for a walk or exercising, I started eating. Suddenly, I felt calm, and it dawned on me that the chewing really calmed my emotions, which reminded me of a class I had taken years ago where they covered some emotional issues that people in the class were experiencing, and we were told we were not allowed to chew gum because it calmed our emotions. Wow, what an "aha" moment that was for me. Suddenly, I understood why I turned to food when I was stressed and upset at work, and why I stuffed down my emotions with the food. It calmed me. It was a huge moment for me. I was constantly learning lessons along the way. However, after that episode, I knew I just *had* to get away from that toxic environment. I was sick and tired of the constant belittling and nastiness. I had had enough.

I had spent thousands and thousands of dollars trying to get out of nursing and trying desperately to find something else to do. I had attended workshops, seminars, self-help conferences. I had spent thousands of dollars on books, CD's, DVD's, self-help and personal development, and yet it had not helped me become the confident person these courses promised. I had paid thousands of dollars to coaches to try and help improve my confidence, and all to no avail. All it left us was debt. I loathed myself for putting my husband through financial stress while I was trying to work on my insecurities. But there were lessons there for me as well. I think I was just a slow learner!

I left that surgery center, and then for the next seven years, while going from the "frying pan into the fire" by moving to other surgery centers and finding that there were bullies in each place, I finally decided that it was enough. I was worn out, broken and so tired. But I learned yet another valuable lesson, that there would always be nurses who are threatened by someone who has a lot of experience. I should have just ignored them, instead I allowed them to send me back into that dark place.

As a child and young girl, my friends used to always describe me as "fun-loving, funny, and bubbly." Now I wondered where this jovial, fun-loving person had gone to. What had happened to me? I grew up in a Christian home. My parents were devout Christians, serving the Lord all their lives. I attended Sunday school and church at boarding school. However, the next years in Cape Town at nursing school, work, and the first five years here, I strayed from the church and definitely God. I am not proud about it, but it is a fact. I am sure that added to my feelings of being lost and not fully belonging.

After we got married, I joined my husband's church. I have no doubt in my mind that attending and serving in our church, attending Bible studies, reading many Christian books and my Bible, and a lot of prayer got me through those hard years first with our family and then my extremely difficult years at work. It had taken a long time, but I was starting to learn about myself and the "stuff" that had held me back for most of my life.

CHAPTER 6

The Stuff That Holds Us Back

Each of us is very different, and not all the same things hold us back. In my searches over the years, I have learned a number of interesting things about myself growing up.

To keep our nurse's license current, we have to take a certain number of educational classes every two years. This can be done by reading certain accepted medical books and classes, certifications, and seminars. I have attended many seminars of interest to me, many which I believe have shed some light on the psychological "baggage" I was holding onto.

I have also prayed for God to open up my eyes to be able to see what has held me back so I can understand, resolve the issues, or accept the reasons and put them behind me and move on as a confident, beloved child of God. Sin, for one, holds us back, and I have prayed for forgiveness for it.

One issue I had was those deep-down feelings of being unworthy and not good enough. I have never felt pretty enough and clever enough, always unsure of myself, lesser than others, dirty. People have often commented on my lack of confidence. I have spoken about my issues so much in this book because at times, they became almost incapacitating.

One of the things I learned from attending seminars is that we can be held back by our own negative "core beliefs." Core beliefs are beliefs we hold deep down, that we assume are truths about ourselves. They aren't necessarily true or factual at all, but we perceive them as absolute facts and truths. These can be negative beliefs responsible for our feelings of insecurity, self-doubt, and need for external validation.

I also learned that core beliefs are so ingrained that they become automatic thoughts, manifesting in symptoms of severe self-criticism, guilt, procrastination, indecisiveness (I'm a master at that!), withdrawal, feelings of not belonging, failure, that if I can't be perfect, I shouldn't try anything, and many more. For me, this is a work in progress because these beliefs, although false, are so deeply ingrained in my subconscious. But, of course, the truth is that God created us all lovingly for a purpose on this earth. Therefore, we *are* good enough, clever enough, pretty enough, and worthy enough and not the above-mentioned feelings and beliefs I had. Now that we know that these core beliefs are absolutely false, we can all learn from this and remember this.

We all know that our thoughts lead to feelings, and our feelings lead to actions. In turn, our actions lead to the results we get in our lives. And this taught me why I wasn't getting the results I so longed for in my life and why I had run from some of the offers I previously had. It was a huge "aha" moment for me to think that these feelings and thoughts were just lies I had believed. Imagine holding ourselves back because we believe the lies.

We are not alone. I hear about this all the time. In my job, I speak with nurses from all over the country. I recently spoke with two who are both excellent nurses and have degrees, one with a doctorate, and both have been bullied. Both are in the process of wanting to break away from traditional nursing. In fact, one has already. And both now tell me that they have felt this imposter syndrome, this feeling that they are not worthy enough to pursue their dreams and will be "found out" and lose their credibility. This is what bullying can do. It can destroy lives. Young people and children have committed suicide due to bullying. It needs to stop. No one has the right to belittle and bully anyone. It can be crippling, and the more nurses I speak with, the more I hear about how rampant bullying is. Of course, bullying is not only in nursing. It happens in work places and very much in schools. This is so sad, but it did help me knowing that I am not alone in dealing with a toxic work environment.

Another thing I believe that holds us back and keeps us stuck is Satan's lies. The evil one does not want us to get "unstuck." He makes sure he does everything he can to keep us mired in the pit. I wanted to write my book to help young women who are stuck in their own false beliefs, and yet I was stuck for years in the lies I had been told. The longer we stay in that pit, the longer our lives are destroyed. I believe the evil one reinforces those negative core beliefs again and again and again *if* we listen to the false messages we are told.

These messages can come from parents, teachers, friends, and even strangers. The woman who was an attorney who verbally attacked me at that party about being a "second-class citizen" had no idea who I was, and the fact that she felt she needed to demean me was beyond me. The sadness is that I believed her and allowed her insecurities to strengthen my core belief that I was unworthy and would never be good enough. Who would believe my message? Of course, it was not true, but I believed it. And that, dear child of God, is how Satan spreads his lies and keeps us mired in the pit.

At an early stage in my nursing career, I began to build my identity around being a nurse. When I retired from nursing, I believed that I had failed miserably in my career (yet another lie) and felt as if I had lost every bit of my identity as well. It has taken me years to realize and believe that my identity is in being a beloved child of God, not being a nurse, and so is yours. You are a beloved child of God.

As the years went by, the calling I felt to write this book was getting weaker and weaker. My biggest fears were that people I knew would laugh at me and reinforce what others had told me growing up. I continued praying for God to open up my eyes so I could find out why I felt this way.

One day, I was sitting doing my quiet time. I don't remember if I was reading my Bible or one of the many Christian books I constantly read when a thought suddenly jumped into my head. *I wonder if having sick brothers and sisters when we were young made an impact on me? Could it possibly have had an effect on my self-esteem or caused a lack of confidence?* That thought came out of the blue. Could this be an answer to my prayers? I wondered. I believe it was. Later that day, I did a bit of research and was amazed to find some literature that confirmed my thoughts. Reading some articles about children growing up with sick siblings, I found out a few things that really helped me. I read that when a child gets very ill, it disrupts and can engulf the entire family, changing their lives. We know that. But I did not know all the possible ramifications. We were so fortunate to have our loving grandparents living close to us on the farm to help us and enable us to stay on the farm, but our mom was away with Tom for fifteen weeks when he was ill with cancer, and Dad was gone for nine of those. It was wonderful to have my grandparents there with us but still very difficult for the entire family.

There were no childhood support experts in those days, and I wonder how much my mom and dad told us about Tom. Was it enough? And yet, how would they know? It was all new to my parents, and one cannot imagine how difficult it was for them. It must have been overwhelming, especially for my mom because she came back with Tom and still had the four of us kids to take care of. Later, she wrote in her book that she was so grateful to have her strong faith. I know it got her through all the dark times.

I read further that siblings of sick children might have feelings of not belonging or guilt because their sister or brother is sick and they wonder why they aren't sick instead.

They also might have feelings of jealousy, due to the sick child getting so much attention. The one article I
read said this can especially happen at the ages of 3-6 years.[1] My twin Stephen and I were four years old, Mary was six, and Jane was eight when Tom was so ill with cancer. Such a difficult age for us all. So much for a family to have to cope with. The article went on to say that typical feelings for siblings of a sick child is to want everything to be normal. And of course, life cannot be "normal." I have asked my sisters if they remember much, and they don't. It was really good to look into this, and although I don't remember any such feelings at all, I do believe that it had to be hard for the four of us to really comprehend the extent of Tom's illness and how desperately ill he was.

Stephen and I were eight years old when Stephen went to hospital for his broken leg. I have often wondered if it was then that I might have felt left behind or possibly guilty that it happened to him and not me. Just learning that these feelings are normal and how it was naturally tough for our whole family and how everyone processes and copes with sickness so differently really helped me. And I do believe we can learn from these tough times and that talking about it would definitely have helped me. But we are all different, and there is not one solution for everyone.

Looking into this also answered thoughts that I had had that my mom didn't love me or care for me. Of *course,* my mom loved me. Of *course,* my mom cared for me. She adored us all.

I know that the calling for writing this book stems from a lot of the "stuff" that has held me back. This is why I feel so strongly about talking to our children, our parents, and our siblings. For me, it answered so many questions I had buried deep down in my subconscious. Having these questions answered for me opened my eyes and helped me understand my many "why's," and I believe it has helped free me to become the person God created me to be.

One more thought that popped up into my heart after praying one night was, can nicknames cause children to suffer low self-esteem later on in life? Once again, I read a few articles about that and was amazed to find out that nicknames or calling your children negative names can have a very profound effect on children. One article answered my question immediately. The article said that "Labelling your child negatively can be the worst thing a loved one can do for their self-worth and their confidence." [2] Wow! I was *shocked!* If you recall, I mentioned earlier that a very close and beloved family member had started calling me a nickname I hated. I don't remember how long it went on for, but I know it affected me for a long time. Was this the reason why I grew up feeling ugly, dirty, and unworthy? Was this why I always wanted to be beautiful? I know that person did not intend to be mean, and of course I have forgiven the beloved person and moved on. I am just grateful because I fully believe that prayer helped me discover this, work it out, and finally understand where some of those feelings came from.

The last thing I want to mention to you about the stuff I believed held me back is this. I continued reading and praying for God to answer some of my questions. One day, I was reading a book called *Overcoming Fear* by Margaret Feinberg. It had sat on my bookshelf for years, and when I eventually brought it out and started reading it, I wondered just why I had allowed it to sit there for so long! One of the chapters was titled "Facing the Fear of Rejection." Okay, I know we all face rejection at times in our lives. But as Margaret Feinberg wrote, "If left unchecked, you might find fear of rejection springing up in your life. You may not want to reach out as much anymore." [3] And I believe that is exactly what happened to me. In my life, I have felt a lot of rejection, and I think it became such an issue that subconsciously, I was too afraid to stand up to the nicknames and bullying at work because I was so scared of being rejected again.

I have not spoken with a psychologist about this or had counseling, but I know it has held me back so many times in my life. I believe that I accepted the name-calling and nasty treatment because of fear of rejection. Understanding this has helped me so much. I am slowly learning to stand up for myself. I still struggle with fear of rejection a lot, thoughts of what other people are thinking about me, but I have really worked on this aspect in my life, and it has helped me immensely. And to think that the book was sitting there in my bookshelf for all those years waiting to be read!

God has a plan for every one of us, and I guess it was time for me to read it then to finally "get it" and be able to understand many of my actions in the past. It all makes so much sense to me now. I am not a psychologist or a therapist, and I will never try and solve another person's problems. All I can do is listen to you, pray for you, and show you how I believe God has guided me and answered all my questions.

My mom wrote in her Bible, which my siblings gave me when she passed away, "Faith plus prayer equals power." She would know. She had such a hard life, but she never *wavered* in her strong faith nor her constant prayers. And that is the kind of faith we need to have. Unwavering.

Child of God, *never* allow *anyone* to tell you that you are not good enough. Who are *they* to tell you that? God put each and every one of us on this earth. He created us in His image because He loves us. He created us for a reason. No one can take that away from us. We are all children of God, loved and adored. *Never* forget that, and *never* let *anyone* take that away from you. We all have different issues that can hold us back. Some can be smaller; some can be debilitating.

My low self-esteem became almost debilitating to me, and yours may be much worse. But I know that I made my mistake by looking in the wrong places for answers. Instead of turning to God and praying for answers, I looked for answers from the self-help and personal development coaches. I believe that I was working on my "outside," spending those years and all that money trying to fix the "outside." I was not fixing nor understanding what was really holding me back on the inside. I looked to others instead of looking to God. When I spent time in prayer and quiet time with God, I got the answers I was looking for. I know that turning to Him is what helped me and now know it could have saved us thousands of dollars and many years spent feeling lost.

Immersing myself into Christian-focused writings, Bible studies, and church has helped me believe that I am a child of God, He loves me, and I am forgiven, worthy, and precious. And so are you.

I now understand some of the missing pieces where I misunderstood people and perceived and believed situations that were not true. It has freed me more than I can say and has brought me to a place where I understand what happened and am finally able to "get it."

CHAPTER 7

"Getting It," Getting Unstuck, and Picking Up the Pieces

Once I got clarification about some things that had occurred in my past and began to understand why they had happened, I started to comprehend why I felt and believed the way I did. Little by little, the nasty memories started fading. Memories that no longer saddened me and definitely did not serve me along with the hurt I was holding onto slowly disappeared. I believe that if we hold onto people who have hurt us and those memories that are negative and destructive, we are held hostage by them. We remain in the pit, and they hold all our God-given power. They don't care and have long forgotten, and yet, this can hold us back for years. I know. It held me back most of my life. I have forgiven the people who hurt me along the way, and there is nothing more freeing than to forgive and be forgiven. And I pray for forgiveness every day.

In picking up the pieces, I want to remind you how I was able to find out what was holding me back and work through those issues and memories and how it changed my life. What was so hard initially became so clear to me, and getting that clarity helped me with moving on. I will say unequivocally that I know it was through prayer that God opened my eyes to my issues, and through being able to "plug into His power," I was able to forgive and move on, walking away from things and people who no longer served me.

I spent most of my life looking to others for validation, but I was looking in all the wrong places. I spent all that money trying to fix my outside when I should have been working on my inside. I was looking for solutions from other people when I should have looked to God for answers. He is the one who validates us. We are His beloved children, and we do not need further validation.

As mentioned earlier, I tied my entire identity to nursing. When I left at the end of my career, I felt broken. My identity is not my nursing. My identity is that I am a precious child of God, and no one can take that from me. And the same is true for you. No matter what someone says about you, the fact that you are a child of God is all the validation you will ever need.

When I turned to food to calm and comfort me, it was the worst vice I could have turned to. I was so out of control with my eating, and my weight yo-yoed up and down for *years*, and not only was it bad for my health, it was devastating to my confidence and invited all sorts of bullying, nastiness, and meanness from people at work. When I allowed bullies to almost destroy every bit of confidence I had, all I needed to remember as a child of God is that I am who God says I am, not what the bullies said I was. God loves me and made me for a purpose, and He is my strength and power. Bullies have no power over me anymore.

When I allowed people to control me because I was scared of standing up for myself for fear of rejection, all I needed was to remember that Jesus suffered the greatest rejection of all for us. And because of His sacrifice, we get to live with Him in heaven for eternity. It makes my fear of rejection so insignificant now.

I tried for so long to be something and someone I was not because I never felt good enough. It was and is exhausting and so discouraging. When I compared myself with others, I never measured up. I *always* fell short. Trying to be something and someone else, I was never good enough anyway. When I started being the person I was meant to be, it became so much easier. As Rick Warren says, "Nothing is more discouraging than trying to be something you are not."[4] I will add "or someone" to that.

As someone who has been a very private person all my life and one with such a fear of rejection, writing this book has been the hardest thing I have ever done. I am afraid of what some friends and family will think of me after opening up about stuff in my life that I have never told anyone before. Sharing these things makes me feel so vulnerable, and it also opens me up to so much judgement and criticism. But I have plowed on because it is my hope and prayer that this book will help make a difference in your life.

Picking up the pieces has strengthened my self-esteem, and I'm definitely becoming more confident. I still fall back into my old habits, but being aware of them allows me to stop my negative self-critical thoughts and remember who I am. I have to remind myself constantly that I am just as worthy as anyone else. I am following what I believe is my calling, and when bad days happen and I feel like I am falling back into my old insecure self, I forcefully make myself continue. Those dark days are becoming a thing of the past, and hoping that I might just possibly make a difference in someone's life keeps me going. It has not been easy, and it has taken me years and a lot of work and prayer to pull myself up and out of those self-defeating thoughts and actions and the self-sabotage that has held me back.

We form these subconscious habits, core beliefs, and negative thoughts, and we often don't even realize that we are falling back into them because it is happening subconsciously. It can be a nasty comment, a word someone says, or a picture or statement someone writes on social media that can trigger those devastating thoughts and feelings that plunge us back into that pit. And then all the old thoughts and feelings of inadequacy, unworthiness, and insecurity come creeping back. Sometimes we take a step forward only to then take five back when this happens.

These thoughts have become ingrained habits that may have taken a lifetime to form in our little minds, and we don't have the willpower to break them. They are too ingrained. They need to be replaced over and over and over until the replacement coping mechanisms become our automatic thoughts and behavior. I still fall back into that pit, but I am so much better from where I was before I started on my journey picking up the pieces.

How have I done it? Literally one step at a time by becoming aware of those destructive and debilitating thoughts when they happen. A lot of times, I don't even realize I'm thinking them. I'll pick it up when I start feeling bad about myself or sometimes just when an uneasy feeling creeps in, and it gives me a sense that something just doesn't feel right. Then I ask myself why I am feeling this way, and I work back to find the cause. It is usually a comment someone has made or a conversation I have had with someone who has made me feel that way before. Then I immediately start praying for strength and intentionally change those negative thoughts by repeating affirmations that replace them. I have put up sticky notes with reminders of who I am and how my faith gives me the belief that I am a beloved child of God, precious in His eyes.

By asking myself why I am feeling this way or doing something like over-eating or why a comment by someone has made me feel this way, it brings what's going on into my conscious mind, and I can then consciously deal with the thoughts and feelings. Often, they are unconscious feelings that have been triggered by previous incidences in my life, and I have to reinforce to myself that they are false beliefs and lies and that I will not let them drag me back into my past.

Another way I have worked to change my thoughts and habits is to visualize in my mind, anything that calms me or makes me happy. I love God's creation—the ocean, birds, animals, flowers, mountains, and anything nature. If I find myself getting stressed or upset, I visualize vivid, beautiful scenery like the waves splashing up onto the sand, mist in the trees, flower gardens, or anything I find calming. I have pictures of beautiful oceans, gardens, and misty mountains hanging up in my house, and I will often take a break and look at them, imagining myself in the tranquil scenery, smelling the flowers, hearing the waves crashing. I picture the sounds, wonderful fragrance, and feeling of cool mist on my skin and contemplate the wonders of God's magnificent creation. This definitely helps me break my negative train of thought, and puts me in a better place. The calm I feel also stops me from turning to food to find comfort.

There are other ways we can change our train of thought. Listening to Christian music, praying, and reading the Bible or Christian books helps to pick us up. Exercising or going for a walk is another wonderful way to enjoy God's creation and lift our spirits.

Laughter has also been a wonderful gift God has given me. It has many wonderful benefits, and I cannot imagine how my life would be without it. It has definitely helped me throughout my journey! I always try to find time to laugh a lot every day, even when I'm going through a tough time. Laughter heals us. (Proverbs 17:22 NIV) says, "A cheerful heart is good medicine, but a crushed spirit dries up the bones." Yes, we are even encouraged in the Bible to be cheerful, and I always add laughter to that!

Believe me, I am still a work in progress! My worst times are if I wake up at night and the evil one encourages the chatter in my mind, telling me that I am a failure, lesser, unworthy. That is when I start praying as hard as I can! For me, consciously praying and visualizing God's glorious creation keeps me from going down that destructive path of unworthiness again.

At this time, I want to mention my husband Gerrit. He has been an amazing support for me and has listened to my struggles all these years. I know that there have been many times when the last thing he needed was to hear about my bad days at work and how I was desperate to get out of nursing, but he still listened, and that helped me so much. Sometimes I would get home and tell him I just needed to vent, and he would sit quietly until I was done. He has been amazingly patient with me all these years. He supported me with my calling to write this book, even when we were financially strapped. I have so much gratitude for his love and support as well as him leading me back to the Lord after I had strayed for so many years.

If you need professional help, go and get help from a counselor, pastor, or psychologist. Please get the help you need. There is absolutely no shame in seeking out professional guidance, and they can help you with deep emotional hurt and put you on the road to becoming the confident person you were created to be. I also encourage you to join a church and Bible study group. It really has helped me in my Christian walk.

Reading books by Christian women has also helped me more that I can say. Just knowing that many of them have also been in a dark place and walked a similar walk and seeing how they found strength by leaning on God and handing over their lives to Him has been so helpful. I pray that you will get the support you need and deserve and *never* forget that you are a beloved child of God, as worthy and precious as anyone. Take that step now.

Jesus said, "Come to me, all you who are weary and burdened, and I will give you rest. Take my yoke upon you and learn from me, for I am gentle and humble in heart, and you will find rest for your souls. For my yolk is easy and my burden is light." Matthew 11: 28-30 (NIV)

This is my favorite verse in the Bible. For me, being able to hand it all over to Jesus gives me the peace I so long for. He carries all my sadness, brokenness, sins, and baggage. Oh, what a glorious sense of peace I get when I hand it all over to Him!

Sometimes what is hardest for us to overcome becomes a message of hope for others. I pray that I can bring that message of hope for you now.

CHAPTER 8

Looking Back and Moving Forward

When I started writing this book, I was hoping it would help young women who are struggling with issues in their past that might be holding them back from becoming who and what they want to be, what they dream of becoming, especially if it was lack of confidence or low self-esteem holding them back. This is something I have written about so much in this book, and it's something I obviously feel very strongly about. I was not expecting that it would lead to many personal discoveries for me.

During this time, my mom passed away. This was such a huge loss to our family. But as I have told you, she lived such a full life. It was a very hard life but a life devoted to God and a life from which we have so much to learn. Her strong, undeniable faith carried her right to the end when she finally "fell of her perch." We all miss her so very much but know that we will all see her again when we too "fall off our perches" and go to heaven when we are called home.

As I mentioned earlier, a number of years before she passed away, my eldest sister Jane asked her to write a book. Sadly, she did not complete her book before she was called home. But reading what she was able to complete brought so much clarity to my life and answered so many questions that had really bothered me. Reading her book made me aware that we *have* to ask questions, and we *have* to communicate with our parents. So many misunderstandings could have been cleared up in my life had I spent more time with her and not been afraid to ask her questions.

Speaking with a friend of mine one day, I told her that I was not at all sure that I would complete this book. I was having many doubts about being able to help others. This is my life, so different from others' lives, and people might think my issues were trivial. How could it help someone from quite literally the other side of the world? She told me that if I did not write it, someone hurting out there might miss out and that my experiences could help young people struggling with their own problems, even though they might be different from mine. She told me that just having someone listen to you and hear you can be so valuable; the problems don't have to be the same issues. I vowed then and there that I would always make myself available to listen to anyone who wanted to share about his or her life with me. Just being heard can make such a difference.

As hard as it is, we have to take 100 percent responsibility for our lives and ask the questions ourselves. My mom's generation was different from ours. She was very stoic and very strong, but I had many questions that needed answers. However, if I didn't *ask* her or tell her that I was struggling, how was she to know?

In summary, I have struggled throughout my life with low self-esteem, self-loathing, and shame. I have been a master at self-sabotage and self-defeating behavior regarding not only my career but also my weight. I have spent a lifetime comparing myself with other women. And I *always fell short.* How would I succeed if every time I see a beautiful person, which, of course, is all the time, I felt ugly, lesser, and unworthy? I allowed people to bully me for years. I have been afraid to ask loved ones questions when I was desperate for answers. I spent the past twenty-plus years absolutely miserable in a profession I didn't want to be in, and because I did not feel good enough or worthy of better, I stayed, stuck and miserable.

After attending a Beth Moore Living Proof Event and two Women of Faith events years ago with some friends from work, I decided that I would complete this book. Listening to these women and reading books written by them showed me that they too are not perfect, and they too have sinned and fallen short. That encouraged me so much.

Many times, those voices of insecurity chatted in my head, telling me I was not beautiful like they were and I couldn't speak like they could. But I continued reading, praying, and writing, and little by little, I started to believe that I could be forgiven for the many sins I had committed throughout my life, sins that I had often felt were too bad to be forgiven. Sharon Jaynes, in her book *Take Hold of the Faith You Long For,* wrote, "Oh, I am so thankful for the truth of Jesus that has set me free from the bondage of the lies. No more shame!" [5]

God loves us so much that He knows how many hairs we have on our heads. Jesus stepped in and showed us that our sins are never too bad to be forgiven. Ask, and we will be forgiven.

These women gave me hope that I, a sinner, can also be used by God and that I must not allow my failures or the fear of failure to hold me back, which is something I have allowed for so many years. And that is just the same for you, children of God. Here is a Bible verse that I read constantly to remind me that all I need to do is plug into God's power: "For God did not give us a spirit of timidity, but a spirit of power, of love, and of self-discipline" (2 Tim. 1:7 NIV).

Reading my mom's book opened my eyes enormously and helped me understand just how hard her life had been. She had done her very best, as difficult it was, to take care of my sick siblings and the farm school, especially after losing her mom when we were young and not having her support anymore. I know in my mind I criticized her for not hearing me. Oh, how wrong I was. I never had the opportunity to ask her forgiveness. Prayer has helped me, but it is a lesson I can always share and hopefully help others with. It is so important to forgive and ask for forgiveness. I know without a doubt in my mind that she would have forgiven me had I just sat down and asked her.

I once read a quote by comedian Steve Harvey: "You simply cannot drive forward if you're focused on what's happening in the rear-view mirror." [6] His explanation was that if you are stuck in the past, you cannot focus on the present or achieve your goals in the future. This is so true. If we keep on looking back at our failures, we won't be able to move on. However, for me, by looking back, I was able to work through my issues and failures, which really helped clear many questions I had and taught me many valuable lessons. Many of my beliefs were false and holding me back. Once I worked through those false beliefs with God's help and got clarity, I felt free to pray for forgiveness. I could then turn my eyes forward and focus on my road ahead, leaving my past behind where it belonged.

As Sharon Jaynes said in her book, "We can take hold of the faith we long for and start anew. We have access to God's power, so we no longer need to give ours to others."[7]

I am ashamed of not feeling good enough when God had given me all I ever needed to be the woman He designed me to be. Even though there were times in my life that I possibly misconstrued other's intentions, motives, or behavior, the bottom line is that I wasted half of my life letting *my* insecurities and lack of confidence hold me back.

My prayer is that I can show you that there is always hope, a message that in times when one feels so lost, alone, and hopeless, we have a wonderful, loving God, and He is who we need to turn to. He is all the love and support we need.

When I told my friend Michelle once more that I could not write this book and that I was going to tear it up, she told me, "What I want you to understand is that your pain will result in someone else's gain. Sharing your story will allow you to exorcise those demons of self-doubt and self-sabotage."

I sincerely hope and pray that my "pain will result in your gain," and I can absolutely say without a doubt that immersing myself into writing this book, reading Christian books and the Bible, and praying a lot has definitely exposed those "demons of self-doubt and self-sabotage" and has helped me learn that I am a beloved child of God. I still struggle with doubt at times, but I now know that as a child of God, I am just as worthy as anyone out there. And so are you. *Never* allow anyone to tell you any different.

CHAPTER 9

Coming Full Circle

Coming full circle, I want to say that I am, by nature, a happy person. It might not have appeared to you the reader as such, but I really am. My husband has a wonderful sense of humor, and we laugh a *lot*. We laugh a lot with our kids and our extended family as well. I have always fallen back on laughter and believe in the wonderful healing powers of it.

I think I just went through a very dark time and was stuck there for an extended period. We still found humor along the way, and I always told my husband that there was definitely a "light at the end of the tunnel—only, it was a freight train!" But I knew one day that beautiful sunlight would blast through the end of the tunnel, and of course it did! There have been many good days and many laughs along the way. I just allowed the mucky stuff to keep me down in the pit too long. But I am out of that pit now and feel stronger than I have ever been.

I have learned to say no when asked to do something that I really don't feel aligns with where I want to be in my

Christian walk, and I believe all I have to do is seek God's guidance. "Look to the Lord and His strength; seek His face always." (1 Chronicles 16:11 NIV)

I want to end with a story that I believe will show you what I mean by my "coming full circle" and how it gave me such wonderful closure for that long chapter in my life and has opened my life up for my next chapter. There are so many lessons in this story, and I believe it shows us what a wonderful, loving, and caring God we have.

I went back to South Africa in July 2015 to visit my mom and family. It really was an excuse to see my mom because she was turning ninety on July 19th.

My mom did not like birthdays. She hated any fuss made for her and hated being in the "limelight." She always told me that she was going to run away on her birthday because her friends in the retirement village and assisted living always made a fuss over her on her special day. She did the same for them, but she never liked it done for her, and she always told them too that she was going to run away for the day! Somehow, I felt that I just had to go. This was her ninetieth birthday, and it was going to be special. My two sisters and brother would be there, and I did not want to miss out on this occasion. My husband agreed with me.

A lot of things happened while I was there, which gave me validation that I was meant to be there. First, our beloved Nonini passed away a few days before Mom's birthday. It felt like we had lost our second mother, and I was so glad that I was there with my family when she passed away. Unfortunately, she was in hospital far away, and we were not expecting this, even though we knew she was very ill, so sadly, we were not able to see her before she passed away. I was so sad, but being with our family really helped me. I was not home when my dad passed away a number of years previously and really only got to mourn his loss a year later when my husband and I were in Cape Town. That was really hard for me. Being there with my family when Nonini passed away helped me a lot.

We had a lovely luncheon for my mom on her birthday. We all went to church together, and then to Gail's Inn for her luncheon. It was just Mom and our immediate family, and it was wonderful. My siblings and I were all staying at Gail's Inn, and it was the first time we had all been together for a long time. Gail was a close friend of Mom's, and we always stayed there when we visited her. It was a lovely old home converted into an inn. Gail is an amazingly generous and warm person, and she spoiled us so much every time we stayed there.

A few days before I arrived in South Africa, my mom had apparently seen her doctor because she said her leg was swelling up in the evenings, and there was an area where the veins were hurting her. Her doctor gave her some sort of gel to rub on her leg and told her she had a varicose vein that might be inflamed. A few days later, my mom told us that her foot was hurting her, and her toes were somewhat swollen, so my sister and I took her back to her doctor. He told her that she had an infection between her toes and gave her some Betadine ointment to put on it. We asked her to watch it closely, and that if it did not clear up her toes and foot, she needed to get a second opinion.

I came back to the US a few days later. My trip took a couple of days, and as soon as I was back, I called her to ask if her foot had improved. Jane was still with her, taking care of her, and told me that it was worse and that my mom's foot and toes were very swollen and hurting her. I asked Jane to take a picture of Mom's foot and text it to me. I was horrified at how swollen her foot had gotten in just those two days.

That night, I went to bed and lay there for ages, praying for my mom. I was so worried about her foot. I eventually fell asleep and woke up a couple of hours later with a jolt, and immediately, a question popped into my head. (I believe that it was an answer to my prayers.) What if her doctor had misdiagnosed her condition and it was her circulation and not an infection?

I called her as soon as I woke up, and my sister told me her foot and toes were very swollen and painful and the tops of two of them were getting discolored. I asked her to feel both Mom's feet. Were they both the same temperature, or was the swollen one cooler? Jane told me it was a "lot cooler." I suddenly had a sick feeling in my stomach. What if the doctor had possibly misdiagnosed her symptoms completely? The fact that her foot was really swollen and cool told me, a nurse, that it meant circulation. I had worked with many vascular surgeons when I came to the United States, as well as some in South Africa, and we saw a lot of patients with blocked arteries in their legs. *Wow, why did I not think about this sooner?* I wondered. I was *so* mad with myself. I told Jane that she needed to get Mom to see a vascular surgeon *immediately*. They went to see the specialist the next day, who confirmed my fears. He told my sister that she had a blockage in the artery leading to her foot. *How on earth could her GP have missed this?*

My sister asked the specialist if he could operate and unblock it. He told her that they could not operate on Mom's leg because her heart was not strong enough to withstand a general anesthetic. When she asked him what they could do to help her, he told them to "take her home and love her."

I was absolutely *shocked*. "*What! Is he insane?*" I all but yelled. "We *cannot* just take her home and love her. Do you have any idea how *excruciating* her foot and leg will get? Do you have any idea how *ghastly* her last days will be? Because we all know this will kill her!" I couldn't even think about how ghastly it would become, couldn't even go there. "He *has* to do something for her, Jane. It will be the worst way for Mom to die. That is *barbaric!* What about a spinal anesthetic? Why can't they do that? We do them all the time here for patients who are too old or too ill to stand a general anesthetic!"

My sister said that this was what he had told her and that he was the specialist. How could she argue. She was not a nurse. I totally agreed. How was she to know? But I was a nurse, and we needed to see what we could do for her. I was in tears by then and *so* angry with myself for not picking up on all this before I had left to come back home. Now I was 10,000 miles away. What could I do?

Once again, I went to bed that night, praying for answers. I lay there for ages, tearful and distraught, trying to think of how we could help her. *Surely* there would be someone who could help her. This was ghastly. What had happened to medicine in South Africa? It used to be so good! I had been gone for twenty-four years and didn't know anyone who would still be practicing in Cape Town, which would be the best place to take her.

Eventually, I fell into a fitful sleep. And once again, God answered my prayers. I woke up with a start a few hours later. I immediately thought about a friend of mine who was living in Sweden. Eric Solomon had married a close friend of mine, Eva, who I had met here in the United States. I had actually introduced them to each other, and they had fallen in love and gotten married! They were both retired and living in Sweden. Eric was the best anesthesiologist I had ever worked with while I was in Cape Town, a brilliant doctor. I knew he had given thousands of patients successful spinal anesthetics and knew that if he had still been practicing in Cape Town, he would have helped Mom. I wondered if he possibly knew a vascular doctor who was still practicing in Cape Town, as well as any good anesthesiologists still in practice. I would call as soon as I woke up the next day and ask all that as well as if he thought it was possible for her to have a spinal anesthetic at her age.

And this is where God orchestrated the next events. Of that, I have no doubt. Eric told me that she could absolutely have a spinal anesthetic and that he knew an anesthesiologist who was still practicing in Cape Town. He would call him that day. I could hardly believe my ears when he told me his name was Dr. Levine. I knew Dr. Levine very well and had worked with him for five years in Cape Town before I came to the United States! What were the chances that he was still practicing?

That day, Eric called Dr. Levine, and he told Eric that he worked with a *very* good vascular surgeon every Thursday. He said to text the photos of my mom's foot to him, and he would show the surgeon the next morning, as they would be working together. Of course, my mom was horrified. She hated a fuss, but I didn't care. We needed to get her to a vascular surgeon as soon as possible. This was an emergency. Eric called me back right away to say that Dr. Levine had spoken with the vascular surgeon and of course they could do a spinal anesthetic for Mom and "sort out her leg," that my sisters must get to her Cape Town immediately.

Mary drove the four hours up to Mossel Bay, where my mom lived, early the next morning while Jane packed my mom's clothes in her room. They knew it was going to be a long stay and that Mom would have to remain with Mary in Cape Town for her surgery and recovery, however long it would take.

Mary drove Mom back to Cape Town on the Sunday. She saw the vascular surgeon on Monday, and he immediately diagnosed her with a blocked artery in her leg. She was added to his surgery schedule for Friday, the soonest he could get her in. By Friday, the tops of her toes were already starting to turn black, and she was in a *lot* of pain. It must have been unbelievably painful. I can't *imagine* what it would have been like days and weeks later.

The next set of crazy circumstances was about to happen—all orchestrated, I know, by our loving Lord. Dr Levine could not do Mom's anesthetic that Friday because he worked with another surgeon on Fridays. But his partner would be there and would take great care of her. Can you just imagine how surprised I was to hear that his partner was Dr. Bean, who just happened to be another anesthesiologist who I had worked with for those five years at the same clinic! And, there was yet another surprise. The nurse who assisted with mom's surgery was a nurse I had also worked with in Cape Town! What were the odds that I had worked with these doctors and the nurse twenty-eight-plus years prior and they *all* happened to be there for Mom now? Just amazing.

My mom had her surgery that Friday afternoon, and during her surgery, she was able to talk to all the staff because she was given the spinal anesthetic. She said that they treated her like "Royalty!" While talking, they also discovered that Dr. Bean had actually spent a night on our farm *many* years previously when he, Eric, and two friends had been hiking in the beautiful Drakensburg Mountains. They had stopped off at our farm and spent the night with Mom and Dad on their way back to Cape Town. Incredible!

Some people would probably say that this was all one huge coincidence, but I do not believe that for one moment. This was all put together by our Lord and was definitely a God-incidence, and of that, I have no doubt. These are those "pieces of the puzzle" Mom wrote about so much in her book.

Mary took her to her home the next day. The artery in her lower leg had been stented, and circulation had been restored to her foot. The surgeon told her that it would take a long time to heal and that she could still possibly lose some of her toes, but she had done exceptionally well, and the doctors were all so impressed with her!

Mary nursed Mom for almost four months, doing her dressings and helping her with all her needs. The black areas on the tops of her toes healed, which is something we did not expect. God was healing her as we prayed. We sure have an amazing God!

I want to tell you the story of how the joke about Mom "falling off her perch" started. Years previously, I would call and wish her a happy New Year on the first of each year. For the past ten years after she turned eighty, she would say that this would be her "last year." The first time she said that, I was so concerned and asked her if there was something wrong with her. She said no but that she had lived past her "three score and ten years" the Bible spoke about, and that each year after that was a bonus year, and she was ready to "fall of my perch" when the Lord called her. At first, I felt very emotional about this, but it became a joke over the next ten years that she had lived beyond what she called her "allotted years plus ten." I know she was lonely and missed my dad, and although very grateful for everything, she was ready to fall off her perch and go to heaven. Toward the end, she would say that she was "praying for our Lord to come and take her home." I know she was really tired. I've heard this so often with my elderly patients.

Anyway, she told me years before that that she was not afraid of dying at all and she welcomed her "time." The *one* thing she didn't want was to die alone. That was her only issue. I don't recall if she actually said she was afraid of dying alone or didn't want to die alone. I was always very concerned about that because I was living here in the US, and both my sisters and brother lived many hours away from her in South Africa. What if she was called home and was alone in her room? The thought used to bother me a lot.

Mom had been with Mary for almost four months and was starting to talk about going back to the assisted living because she felt she was a burden for Mary. I know without a doubt she was not. In fact, Mary treasured this time with Mom. Mary is single, had always been exceptionally close to Mom, and loved having Mom with her. I know Mom treasured the time as well, but she felt guilty about being a burden, even though we all told her it was exactly the opposite.

Toward the end of November just before Thanksgiving, I called Mom to see how she was doing. She sounded so very tired. Mary told me that she thought Mom was going down quickly. She said she was so tired a lot of the time and had no energy. I asked her if she thought she was depressed, and she said no, just very tired.

I called the next day, and Mary said that Mom was not well, and she was very concerned about her. Mom did not want to see a doctor and said she was just tired and ready to go home to be with Jesus.

At about one o'clock on the morning of November 24th, Mom called Mary to her room. She told Mary she thought she was having a heart attack. When asked, she said she was not having any pain but her arms and legs were full of pins and needles. Mary told her she was going to call the ambulance so that they could give her some oxygen, hoping it would make her feel better. Mom did not want Mary to call the ambulance and told her she was not going anywhere in an ambulance! She again said she had no pain. I am sure she knew she was dying and did not want to die in the hospital. Half an hour later, Mom passed away *perfectly* peacefully while Mary gently held her face in her hands, praying with her.

One would think that would have been so frightening and stressful for Mary. She is not a nurse, and holding a person as he or she dies is hard enough for a nurse, let alone someone who has never experienced this, above all, with a precious mother. And yet, Mary, whose faith is as strong as our mom's, said, "We were surrounded by the most indescribable, awesome sense of peace and calm. I have *never* felt like that in my life. It could *only* have been the Lord's presence." I have no doubt that it was our Lord's presence.

The next miracle was that the ambulance did arrive, but they had gotten lost and got there after Mom had gone to be with Jesus. God's timing is always perfect. As Mary said, had they arrived before Mom had gone, she would not have had those precious last moments alone with her, moments that are now equally precious memories. Mary also said that the paramedics told her that there was such a "calmness" in her home. Once again, I am reminded of where Mom wrote about that when the orderlies wheeled Tom out of surgery, there was suddenly a calming, warm wind. Even the orderlies mentioned it. The Holy Spirit was there with them, comforting them in their time of need. And I believe it was the same for Mary when Mom slipped away, God's perfect timing once again.

I will say again that I have no doubt in my mind that God orchestrated this all. Mom's one fear or concern about dying was that she did not want to be alone. God made sure of that. He took her to Cape Town, where she spent almost four months with her precious Mary, our sister. I know Mom was lonely where she lived, but she never said as much, other than that she missed us kids. Now she got to spend her last precious months on earth with Mary. Amazing.

Do you see just how God put all the pieces of her puzzle together? Early on in my book when I was writing about Tom's brain cancer and illness, I mentioned that Dad had managed to find a job with that construction company. You will remember that the owner had had brain cancer, and the same surgeon had operated on him. Mom, in her strong faith, wrote that it was, "God's design, putting all the pieces of the puzzle in place." And here once again, I absolutely believe that God was putting the final pieces of her puzzle together. He answered her prayer about her concerns about not wanting to die alone, and she passed away so peacefully in my sister's arms.

And one final thought for me. I now have the belief that because I was a nurse, I was able to pray for and get guidance from God so we were able to get my mom to the surgeon in Cape Town. She died so very peacefully, and the joy of it was that because of her surgery, she did not have a ghastly, painful death.

If for nothing else, I am so grateful that I became a nurse, and because of my contacts along the way, albeit twenty-eight-plus years before, we were, with God's help, *all* able to help put her last "pieces of the puzzle" in place, exactly where they were meant to be. With God's divine guidance, she had such a wonderful, peaceful send-off to heaven to be with Dad, Tom, her parents, her beloved brothers, and all our friends who had gone before her. She was completely aware of what was happening, told Mary she could see Jesus coming to take her home, and then said that she was "going now" as she peacefully slipped away to be with Jesus. We are so grateful to Mary for *all* she did for Mom and that she was there with her as she slipped away to her eternal home. I think it is the most amazing story I have *ever* heard, such a testimony to Mary and our mom's faith.

Do you understand how profound this was? I really feel that my life has come full circle. Mom's last piece of her puzzle had been put in place by our loving Savior. It was complete, and I felt as if I was free now to close that chapter of my life and move on to other things God had been calling me to do. I know Mom would approve!

But before I do go, I have one more message. Wherever we find ourselves in our life's walk, we must give our everything. We can all make a difference in someone's life. We just need to have faith in God. I hope and pray that I helped my patients while being a nurse.

At the end of October 2019, I "hung up my scrubs" for the last time and retired from nursing. I will always be a nurse, just not practice at the bedside. Although I had struggled a lot along the way, I did have many good times and met many wonderful people, making many close friends along the way. I am lucky and very grateful for that. And in the end, being a nurse served me well. Now it was time to pass the baton to another younger nurse and move on to other horizons. My life has certainly come full circle, and I am looking forward to what our Lord has in store for me for the next years until I too "fall off my perch" and join Mom, Dad, Tom, our family, and friends in paradise.

And in saying this, I have a few last things to say to you, beloved child of God. You might be struggling with all the "stuff" life throws at you—pain, burdens, shame, sadness, and struggles. Life can be so harsh and sometimes ghastly. Please understand that being a committed Christian does not mean that your life is going to be perfect and smooth sailing. It doesn't mean that you won't be abused or bullied. The world is full of sin and evil. My mom had such a hard life, but her faith kept her so strong, and she never let life beat her down. She once wrote a letter to me when I was really struggling. I had made some changes and decisions in my life but felt that they were wrong and was agonizing about them and struggling with letting go. She said in her letter encouraging me, "I have made *lots* of changes in my life, and never mourned a single one. I just pulled down the curtain and *happily* moved on." Oh, that I could have listened to her so many years ago when she wrote this. It could have saved me so much heartache in my past! But we can all learn from her. Life is going to throw so much at us, and we will have to be strong, make decisions, and make changes, some of which won't work. But we can learn from her and be strong and lean on God for that strength, just as she did.

Just as I sifted through my past, praying for God to open up my eyes to what I had struggled with, I pray that you will be able to do the same. My issues might be completely different from yours, but I found so many answers when I prayed about them, asking God for guidance. He has never let me down and promises us that He will never leave us nor forsake us.

Maybe you have some false core beliefs that you are holding on to, and they, in turn, are holding you back from becoming the beautiful child God created you to be. Maybe you were bullied or abused and cannot let go of the shame. Maybe you were the sibling of a very sick child and grew up feeling guilty that you were healthy or felt that you were forgotten and left behind. Maybe you had a very critical or harsh parent, teacher, or husband and you never felt good enough. Maybe you feel swallowed up by your pain, guilt, or shame. It doesn't matter how broken we or our lives are; Jesus forgives us.

Every little girl needs to grow up knowing in her heart that she is loved, valued, and born with a purpose for Him. If your life hasn't felt like that before or you have not known this, know and believe it now. We are *all* beloved children of God.

Whatever the reason, I hope and pray that you get the help you need so that you can be freed from the chains that bind you to your past and be free to move ahead and become the strong, confident person God created you to be.

I am still very much a novice in my walk with our Lord, but it is my hope and prayer that I can pass on to you that we have an awesome, loving, forgiving God who can bring you comfort and hope. Know and believe in your heart that you never have to feel ugly, less than, smaller, inferior, or not good enough. Never let anyone tell you that you are not good enough. You no longer need to remain swallowed up by the darkness as long as you remember Jesus is with us every minute of the day, every step of the way.

And, precious child of God, we have *all* been given a light to shine. Never let *anyone* dim your light. It is a gift from God. Put your trust in Him, plug into His power, follow your calling, and *shine* your beautiful light.

About the Author

Carol Lumsden was born in South Africa and raised on a farm. Because of the farm's remote location, she and her four siblings went to boarding school at a young age. A painfully shy child who lacked confidence, she struggled at times while at boarding school as she was bullied and unable to stop it due to her low self-esteem and fear of rejection.

After school, Carol moved to Cape Town to study to become a nurse. Although her nursing career was at times rewarding, she still struggled with low self-esteem and lack of confidence and once more encountered a lot of bullying, which she has now found out is fairly common in the nursing profession. She has often felt that she was in the wrong profession and did attempt other careers but felt she was never good enough, pretty enough, or worthy enough, and ultimately gave up her dreams and went back into nursing.

Carol has retired from nursing and is pursuing a career as a Writer and Speaker, working to help women of all ages learn to believe that they are all precious children of God, loved unconditionally and just as worthy as anyone else.

Carol and her husband Gerrit live in Southern California near to their family and three precious grandsons.

How to contact Carol: Email: Carol.Lumsden@aol.com
Phone: (909) 949-0333
Website: www.CarolLumsdenVL.com

Endnotes

1 https://www.webmd.com/palliative-care/siblings-of-children-with-serious-illnesses?print=true

2 https://flintboxcom/blog/parenting/why-name-calling-your-child-is-a-big-no-no

3 Margaret Feinberg, *Overcoming Fear* (Nashville, Tennessee: Thomas Nelson, Inc., 2007). 34

4 https://pastorrick.com/be-who-god-created-you-to-be/

5 Sharon Jaynes, *Take Hold of the Faith You Long For* (Grand Rapids, MI: Baker Books, 2016).

6 https://fearlessmotivation.com/2018/01/31/steve-harvey-quotes-rules/

7 Sharon Jaynes, *Take Hold of the Faith You Long For* (Grand Rapids, MI: Baker Books, 2016).